Professional CSS3

Harness the power of CSS3 to design stunning, modern websites

Piotr Sikora

BIRMINGHAM - MUMBAI

Professional CSS3

First published: May 2016

Production reference: 1260516

Published by Packt Publishing Ltd.
Livery Place
35 Livery Street
Birmingham B3 2PB, UK.

ISBN 978-1-78588-094-0

www.packtpub.com

Credits

Author
Piotr Sikora

Reviewer
Ed Wheeler

Commissioning Editor
Priya Singh

Acquisition Editor
Prachi Bisht

Content Development Editor
Rashmi Suvarna

Technical Editor
Shivani K. Mistry

Copy Editors
Sameen Siddiqui
Roshni Banerjee

Project Coordinator
Judie Jose

Proofreader
Safis Editing

Indexer
Hemangini Bari

Graphics
Abhinash Sahu

Production Coordinator
Melwyn Dsa

Cover Work
Melwyn Dsa

About the Author

Piotr Sikora is lead frontend developer at Nitro Digital, based in Kielce, Poland. He started working on web projects when he was in high school. Over the years, he has been a Flash developer, project manager, and team supervisor. He loves digital projects and dealing with all things digital.

Piotr is a b-boy (break dancer) and has learned a lot of artistic stuff from dance. He teaches dance in his free time.

I would like to thank my wife and daughter for giving me great inspiration and motivating me to write this book. I also give deep thanks to my parents, who always supports me.

I would also like to thank all my friends and mentors that I've had over the years — mentors such as Wojciech Świderski of the Apollo13 team who showed me how to think in CSS and JavaScript; Krzysztof Łosiak of Reborn team for first web ideas and knowledge sharing; the Nitro Digital team for their support, cooperation and still new possibilities; the Broken Glass 2 crew for providing inspiration, creative and open-minded thinking. Without you guys, writing this book would have been impossible!

About the Reviewer

Ed Wheeler works as a frontend developer focused on building reusable and scalable interfaces for websites. With over 10 years of experience in building frontend code, Ed has helped small, medium, and large organizations alike. Ed has also been the technical reviewer for Packt Publishing's video series *Mastering CSS*.

www.PacktPub.com

eBooks, discount offers, and more

Did you know that Packt offers eBook versions of every book published, with PDF and ePub files available? You can upgrade to the eBook version at www.PacktPub.com and as a print book customer, you are entitled to a discount on the eBook copy. Get in touch with us at customercare@packtpub.com for more details.

At www.PacktPub.com, you can also read a collection of free technical articles, sign up for a range of free newsletters and receive exclusive discounts and offers on Packt books and eBooks.

https://www2.packtpub.com/books/subscription/packtlib

Do you need instant solutions to your IT questions? PacktLib is Packt's online digital book library. Here, you can search, access, and read Packt's entire library of books.

Why subscribe?

- Fully searchable across every book published by Packt
- Copy and paste, print, and bookmark content
- On demand and accessible via a web browser

Table of Contents

Preface

CSS is often perceived as a simple language. In fact, while being declarative and apparently simple, it is pretty hard to maintain. For a growing large-scale web application, maintainability is crucial. This book is about ways to leverage known tricks and hacks, new CSS level 3 module techniques, preprocessors, and other tools to create really high-quality products. This will include examples on techniques such as float handling and component-based CSS.

What this book covers

Chapter 1, *Foundations and Tools*, is about the tools that will help you build better CSS code. It describes the features of preprocessors before providing foundational knowledge about SASS. In this chapter, you will get basic knowledge about automatization of repeatable processes in frontend development with GULP.js. You will also find an example of file structures, which you can use to divide a project into files that are small and easy to edit and maintain.

Chapter 2, *Mastering of Fundamentals*, helps you master the box model, floating CSS, positioning troubleshooting, and display types. After this chapter, you will be more aware of foundations of HTML and CSS.

Chapter 3, *Mastering of Pseudoelements and Pseudoclasses*, describes pseudoclasses and pseudoelements and how you can use them. It will cover the problem of drawing primitives and how to use them as a part of optimized CSS code.

Chapter 4, *Responsive Websites – Prepare Your Code for Specific Devices*, provides knowledge about RWD and how to prepare projects. It will cover problems of modern websites and optimization techniques.

Chapter 5, Using Background Images in CSS, addresses the fact that images are on almost every webpage. This chapter will teach you how to craft an optimal website with images displayed correctly on a wide spectrum of modern devices, including mobile phones and tablets.

Chapter 6, Styling Forms, teaches you about styling forms and which elements of CSS you can and cannot use.

Chapter 7, Resolving Classic Problems, is about troubleshooting classic problems in CSS: dealing with opacity, transforms, and centering elements.

Chapter 8, Usage of Flexbox Transform, teaches you about new features of CSS and where to use them.

Chapter 9, Calc, Gradients, and Shadows, will provide information about calc function, which will help you with math operations in CSS. This chapter will reveal the gradient functions and how can you use them in HTML layouts. In this chapter, you will also get a basic knowledge about CSS shadows and its usage. After this chapter, you will know how to add shadow to boxes and texts.

Chapter 10, Don't Repeat Yourself – Let's Create a Simple CSS Framework, is about building reusable code and how to later use it as a foundation for your own projects. This chapter will cover problems related to creating basic CSS frameworks.

Chapter 11, Mailers Fundamentals, is a short introduction to mailers and problems that can occur during the mailer building process. The chapter is focused on fundamental knowledge.

Chapter 12, Scalability and Modularity, teaches you how to prepare scalable code in CSS.

Chapter 13, Code Optimization, is about the final process that takes place after building CSS code. It's mainly about optimization and minification tools. It covers the problems involved in preparing your code before you start coding and during the creation of CSS code.

Chapter 14, Final Automatization and Processes Optimization, is about the automatization of operations over CSS code.

What you need for this book

To use this book, it is recommended you install your favorite IDE, which should support the following:

- HTML
- SASS
- CSS

For better understanding of the code and its debugging, you will need a browser such as:

- Google Chrome
- Mozilla Firefox
- Internet Explorer 9+

Additionally, you will need the following:

- Ruby (to install SASS)
- SASS
- Node.js (to install Gulp.js)
- Gulp.js

Who this book is for

This book is meant for all frontend developers who want to learn how to use the features of CSS and SASS. The book covers a number of topics that can be interesting for developers at each level. If you are a beginner, it will introduce you to CSS and SASS. If you an intermediate/expert programmer, this book can be a good refresher of some CSS and SASS features. Additionally, the final chapter is for all developers who want to start working as a frontend developer and want to automatize a bunch of tasks such as the minification of CSS code.

Conventions

In this book, you will find a number of tools. Mainly it will be SASS and CSS code but as you know CSS is not working by itself and we will be using basic HTML structures. Additionally there will be a bunch of JS code which will describe Gulp.js taks.

Code words in text, database table names, folder names, filenames, file extensions, pathnames, dummy URLs, user input, and Twitter handles are shown as follows: "With preprocessor, each @import makes a merging for you, and in this place you will have a content of mentioned file "

A block of code is set as follows:

```
@import "typography.css"
@import "blocks.css"
@import "main.css"
@import "single.css"
```

Any command-line input or output is written as follows:

```
npm init
npm install gulp-compass gulp --save-dev
```

New terms and **important words** are shown in bold. Words that you see on the screen, for example, in menus or dialog boxes, appear in the text like this: "The easiest way to invoke inspector is to right-click on an element and choose **Inspect** ."

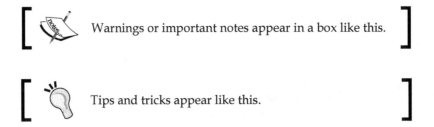

Warnings or important notes appear in a box like this.

Tips and tricks appear like this.

Reader feedback

Feedback from our readers is always welcome. Let us know what you think about this book—what you liked or disliked. Reader feedback is important for us as it helps us develop titles that you will really get the most out of.

To send us general feedback, simply e-mail feedback@packtpub.com, and mention the book's title in the subject of your message.

If there is a topic that you have expertise in and you are interested in either writing or contributing to a book, see our author guide at www.packtpub.com/authors.

Customer support

Now that you are the proud owner of a Packt book, we have a number of things to help you to get the most from your purchase.

Downloading the example code

You can download the example code files for this book from your account at `http://www.packtpub.com`. If you purchased this book elsewhere, you can visit `http://www.packtpub.com/support` and register to have the files e-mailed directly to you.

You can download the code files by following these steps:

1. Log in or register to our website using your e-mail address and password.
2. Hover the mouse pointer on the **SUPPORT** tab at the top.
3. Click on **Code Downloads & Errata**.
4. Enter the name of the book in the **Search** box.
5. Select the book for which you're looking to download the code files.
6. Choose from the drop-down menu where you purchased this book from.
7. Click on **Code Download**.

You can also download the code files by clicking on the **Code Files** button on the book's webpage at the Packt Publishing website. This page can be accessed by entering the book's name in the **Search** box. Please note that you need to be logged in to your Packt account.

Once the file is downloaded, please make sure that you unzip or extract the folder using the latest version of:

- WinRAR / 7-Zip for Windows
- Zipeg / iZip / UnRarX for Mac
- 7-Zip / PeaZip for Linux

The code bundle for the book is also hosted on GitHub at `https://github.com/PacktPublishing/Professional-CSS3`. We also have other code bundles from our rich catalog of books and videos available at `https://github.com/PacktPublishing/`. Check them out!

Downloading the color images of this book

We also provide you with a PDF file that has color images of the screenshots/
diagrams used in this book. The color images will help you better understand the
changes in the output. You can download this file from `http://www.packtpub.com/
sites/default/files/downloads/ProfessionalCSS3_ColorImages.pdf`.

Errata

Although we have taken every care to ensure the accuracy of our content, mistakes
do happen. If you find a mistake in one of our books—maybe a mistake in the text or
the code—we would be grateful if you could report this to us. By doing so, you can
save other readers from frustration and help us improve subsequent versions of this
book. If you find any errata, please report them by visiting `http://www.packtpub.
com/submit-errata`, selecting your book, clicking on the **Errata Submission Form**
link, and entering the details of your errata. Once your errata are verified, your
submission will be accepted and the errata will be uploaded to our website or added
to any list of existing errata under the Errata section of that title.

To view the previously submitted errata, go to `https://www.packtpub.com/books/
content/support` and enter the name of the book in the search field. The required
information will appear under the **Errata** section.

Piracy

Piracy of copyrighted material on the Internet is an ongoing problem across all
media. At Packt, we take the protection of our copyright and licenses very seriously.
If you come across any illegal copies of our works in any form on the Internet, please
provide us with the location address or website name immediately so that we can
pursue a remedy.

Please contact us at `copyright@packtpub.com` with a link to the suspected
pirated material.

We appreciate your help in protecting our authors and our ability to bring you
valuable content.

Questions

If you have a problem with any aspect of this book, you can contact us at
`questions@packtpub.com`, and we will do our best to address the problem.

1
Foundations and Tools

It is important to learn about the foundations in each area. You need to have basic information to be a professional. Good usage of tools is almost as important as the foundation. Without good tools, your foundation won't be used well.

This chapter is about tools that will help to build better CSS code. It describes features of preprocessors and finally the foundation knowledge about SASS. In this chapter, you can get basic knowledge about automatization of repeatable processes in frontend development with GULP.js. Finally, you can find an example of file structure, which will partialize your project into small, easy to edit, and maintainable files.

In this chapter, we will:

- Learn about the usage of preprocessors.
- Create a CSS project with a proper structure.

Choosing the right IDE

Building CSS code is pretty simple. If you want to start, you just need a simple text editor and start writing your code. If you want to speed up the process, you will need to choose the right text editor or integrated development environment (IDE). Currently the most popular editors/IDEs for frontend developers are as follows:

- Sublime Text
- Atom
- WebStorm/PHPStorm
- Eclipse/Aptana
- Brackets

Your choice will be based on price and quality. You should use the editor that you feel most comfortable with.

Speeding up the programming process with snippets/Emmet

When you are creating a code, you have parts of codes that you repeat in all projects/files. You will need to create snippets that will help you to speed up the process of writing code. As a frontend developer, I recommend you to get a basic knowledge about **Emmet** (previously Zen Coding). This is a collection of HTML/CSS snippets, which will help you build code faster. How to use it? It is basically included in modern frontend editors (Sublime Text, Atom, Brackets, WebStorm, and so on). If you want to check how Emmet works in CSS you need to start a declaration of some class for example `.className`, open the brackets ({}) and write for example:

```
pl
```

Then press the *Tab* button, which will trigger the Emmet snippet. As a result, you will get the following:

```
padding-left
```

Following are examples of the most used properties and values:

Emmet form	Result
bg	Background
bgc	Background color
m	Margin
ml, mr, mt, mb	Margin-left, margin-right, margin-top, margin-bottom
ml20px	Margin-left: 20px
c	Color
fl	Float: left
p20px20p	Padding: 20px 20%
tac	Text-align: center
tdn	Text-decoration: none
ttu	Text-transform: uppercase
dib	Display: inline-block
!	!important

For a better understanding of Emmet and to get a full list of features, it is recommended to check the official website of the project at: `http://emmet.io/`.

Keyboard shortcuts

Do you remember when you learned the most impressive keyboard shortcuts *Ctrl + C ,Ctrl + V*? It helped you to save about 2 seconds each time you wanted to make an operation of copying and pasting some text or any other element. But what about automizing some processes in building code? Yeah, it's going to be helpful and you can do it with keyboard shortcuts.

Shortcuts that you should know in your IDE are as follows:

- Duplicating line
- Deleting line
- Moving line
- Formatting code

Cross browser compatibility – which browsers should you install?

To test your code, you will need all the modern web browsers. In your list, you should have the following browsers:

- Google Chrome (newest version)
- Mozilla Firefox (newest version)
- Mozilla Firefox developers edition (newest version)
- Opera (newest version)
- Safari (newest version)
- Internet Explorer

Internet Explorer (IE) is the biggest issue in frontend developers' lives because you will need a bunch of IEs on your machine, for example, 9, 10, and 11. The list is getting smaller because back in the days the list was longer. IE6, 7, 8, 9, and so on. Now IE6, 7, and 8 are mostly not supported by the biggest web projects like YouTube and Facebook. But it sometimes occurs in big companies in which the changing of operating systems is a pretty complicated process.

To easily test your code on a bunch of browsers, it is good to use online tools dedicated for this test:

- `https://crossbrowsertesting.com/`
- `https://www.browserling.com/`
- `https://www.browserstack.com/`

But an easy and free way to do it is to create a virtual machine on your computer and use the system and browser which you need. To collect the required versions of IE, you can refer to `http://modern.ie`. With `modern.ie`, you can select the IE version you need and your version of virtual machine platform (VirtualBox, Parallels, Vagrant, VMware).

How to use inspector

Dealing with HTML and CSS code is almost impossible nowadays without inspector. In this tool, you can see the markup and CSS. Additionally, you can see the box model. This is well known too in browsers for web developers. A few years ago, everybody was using Firebug dedicated for Firefox. Now each modern browser has its own built-in inspector, which helps you to debug a code.

The easiest way to invoke inspector is to right-click on an element and choose **Inspect**. In Chrome, you can do it with a key shortcut. In Windows, you have to press *F12*. In MAC OSX, you can use *cmd + alt + I* to invoke inspector.

Key shortcuts

For faster using of your browser, it's good to know some key combinations that will speed up the process.

Key combination	Function
Ctrl + R, cmd + R	Reload
Ctrl + Shift + R, cmd + shift + R	Reload with cache
cmd + I, F12	Inspector
Ctrl + U, cmd + alt + U	Source of page

Preprocessor – why should you use them?

A preprocessor is a program that will build CSS code from other syntax similar or almost identical to CSS. The main advantages of preprocessors are as follows:

- Code nesting
- Ability of using variables
- Ability of creating mixins
- Ability of using mathematical/logical operations
- Ability of using loops and conditions
- Joining of multiple files

Nesting elements in preprocessors

Preprocessors give you the advantage of building code with nesting of declarations. In simple CSS, you have to write the following:

```
.class {
  property: value;
}
.class .insideClass {
  property: value;
}
```

In the preprocessor, you just need to write the following:

```
.class {
  property: value;
```

```
    .insideClass {
      property: value;
    }
}
```

Or in SASS with the following indentation:

```
.class
  property: value

  .insideClass
    property: value
```

And it will simply compile to code:

```
.class {
  property: value;
}
.class .insideClass {
  property: value;
}
```

The proper usage of nesting will give you the best results. You need to know that good CSS code.

Using variables to parametrize your CSS code

In good CSS code, there is no possibility to use variables in all browsers. Sometimes you are using same value in the few places, but when you have change requests from client/project manager/account manager, you just immediately need to change some colors/margins, and so on. In CSS, usage of variables is not supported in old versions of Internet Explorer. Usage of variables is possible with CSS preprocessors.

Using mixins in preprocessors

In classic programming language, you can use functions to execute some math operations or do something else like displaying text. In CSS, you haven't got this feature, but in preprocessors you can create mixins. For example, you need prefixes for border-radius (old IE, Opera versions):

```
-webkit-border-radius: 50%;
-moz-border-radius: 50%;
border-radius: 50%;
```

You can create a mixin (in SASS):

```
@mixin borderRadius($radius) {
  -webkit-border-radius: $radius;
  -moz-border-radius: $radius;
  border-radius: $radius;
}
```

And then invoke it:

```
@include borderRadius(20px)
```

Mathematical operations

In preprocessors, you can use math operations like the following:

- Addition
- Subtraction
- Multiplying
- Dividing

As an example, we can create simple grid system. You will need, for example, 10 columns with a resolution of 1,000 pixels:

```
$wrapperWidth: 1000px;
$columnsNumber: 10;
$innerPadding: 10px;

$widthOfColumn = $wrapperWidth / $columnsNumber;

.wrapper {
  width: $wrapperWidth;
}

.column {
  width: $widthOfColumn;
  padding: 0 10px;
}
```

Logic operations and loops

Without a logical operator's comparison of operations and loops, you cannot create a good program in classic programming language. The same applies to preprocessors. You need them to automatize the creation of classes/mixins, and so on. The following is the list of possible operators and loops.

The list of comparison operators is as follows:

- `<`: less than
- `>`: greater than
- `==`: equal to
- `!=`: not equal to
- `<=`: less or equal than
- `>=`: greater or equal than

The list of logical operators is as follows:

- `and`
- `or`
- `not`

The list of loops is as follows:

- `if`
- `for`
- `each`
- `while`

Joining of multiple files

In classic CSS, you can import files into one CSS document. But in a browser, it still makes additional requests to the server. So, let's say when you have a file with the following content:

```
@import "typography.css"
@import "blocks.css"
@import "main.css"
@import "single.css"
```

It will generate four additional requests to CSS files. With a preprocessor, each `@import` makes a merging for you, and in this place you will have the content of the mentioned file. So, finally, you have four files in one.

Less – a short introduction

Less is a preprocessor mainly used in a Bootstrap framework. It has all the features of a preprocessor (mixins, math, nesting, and variables).

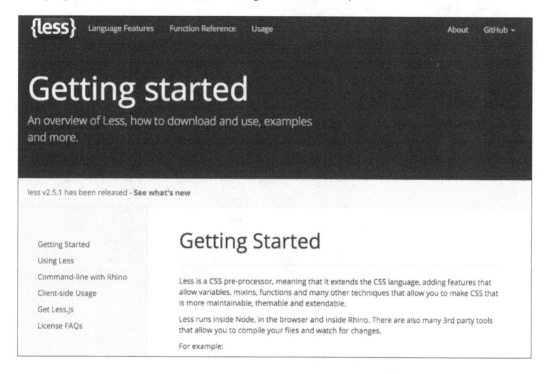

One of the good features is the quick invoking of declared mixins. For example, you have created a class:

```
.text-settings {
  font-size: 12px;
  font-family: Arial;
  text-align: center;
}
```

Then you can add declared properties with its values in other elements declared in your less file (it works like a mixin):

```
p {
  .text-settings;
  color: red;
}
```

You will finally get the following:

```
p {
    font-size: 12px;
    font-family: Arial;
    text-align: center;
    color: red;
}
```

CSS with Stylus

Stylus has two versions of code (like SASS): one with braces/semicolons and the other without braces/semicolons. Additionally (over SASS), you can omit colons. If it continues to be developed and still retains its present features, it's going to be the biggest competitor for SASS.

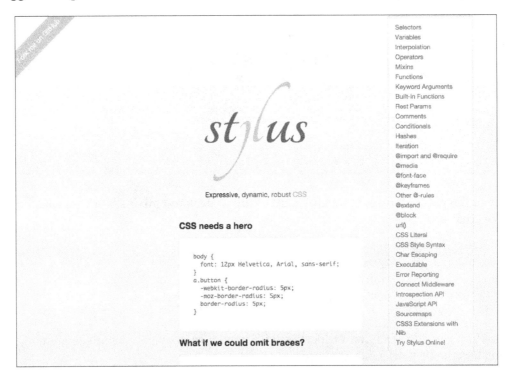

SASS – the most mature preprocessor

SASS stands for **Syntactically Awesome Stylesheets**. It first appeared in 2006 and was mainly connected to **Ruby on Rails (RoR)** projects. Agile methodology used in RoR had an influence on frontend development. This is currently the best known CSS preprocessor used in the Foundation framework with the combination of Compass. A new version of the Twitter Bootstrap (fourth version) framework is going to be based on SASS too.

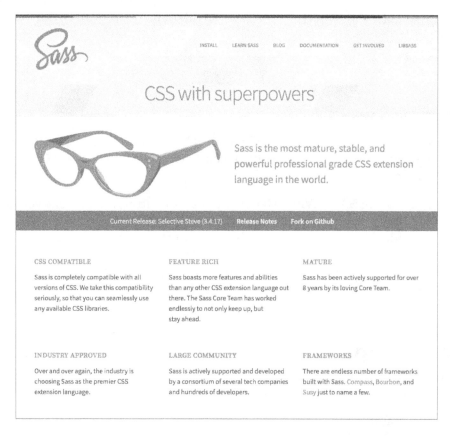

In SASS, you can write code in a CSS-like version called **SCSS**. This version of code looks pretty similar to CSS syntax:

```
a {
  color: #000;

  &:hover {
    color: #f00;
  }
}
```

The second version of code is SASS. It uses indentations and is the same as the preceding code, but written in SASS:

```
a
  color: #000;

  &:hover
        color: #f00;
```

You can see bigger differences in mixins. To invoke a mixin in SCSS, write the following:

```
@include nameOfMixin()
```

To invoke a mixin in SASS, write the following:

```
+nameOfMixin()
```

As you can see, SASS is a shorter version than SCSS. Because of the shortcuts and the automatization processes it is highly recommend to use SASS over SCSS—write Less—get more.

Personally I'm using SASS. Why? The first reason is its structure. It looks very similar to Jade (an HTML preprocessor). Both of them are based on indentation and it is easy stylize Jade code. The second reason is the shorter versions of functions (especially mixins). And the third reason is its readability. Sometimes, when your code is bigger, the nesting in SCSS looks like a big mess. If you want, for example, to change a nested class to be in any other element, you have to change your { }. In SASS, you are just dealing with indentation.

Short comparison

I've been working a lot with Less and SASS. Why did I finally chose SASS? Because of the following reasons:

- It's a mature preprocessor
- It has very good math operations
- It has extensions (Compass, Bourbon)

Usage of Compass is recommended because:

- It has a collection of modern mixins
- It creates sprites

Most preprocessors have the same options and the reason you will choose one is your own preferences. In this book, I will be using SASS and Compass. In the following table, you can find a short comparison:

	Less	Stylus	SASS
Variables	Yes	Yes	Yes
Nesting	Yes	Yes	Yes
Mixins	Yes	Yes	Yes
Math	Yes	Yes	Yes
Additional collections of mixins	No	No	Yes (Compass/ Bourbon)

SASS foundation

Using the SASS preprocessor is really simple. You can use it in two ways: SCSS and SASS itself. Using the SASS preprocessor is really simple. You can use it in two ways: SCSS and SASS. The SCSS syntax looks like extended CSS. You can nest your definitions using new braces. SASS syntax is based on indent (similar for example to Python language).

Variables – where and how to use

Using variables is the essential feature of SASS, which is mostly impossible in CSS that is used on most modern browsers. Variables can be used in every element that you want to parametrize, such as colors, margins, paddings, and fonts.

To define variables in SASS, you just need to do it with the $ sign and add the name of your variable after it.

In SCSS:

```
$color_blue: blue;
```

Usage:

```
.className {
  color: $color_blue;
}
```

Simple mixins – where and how to use (@mixin, @include)

As mentioned in the previous section, variables can be used to parametrize the code. The second best known feature is to add some predefined block of code that you can invoke with some shorter version.

In SCSS, you can predefine it this way:

```
@mixin animateAll($time) {
  -webkit-transition: all $time ease-in-out;
  -moz-transition: all $time ease-in-out ;
  -o-transition: all $time ease-in-out;
  transition: all $time ease-in-out;
}
```

And then invoke with:

```
@include animateAll(5s)
```

In the SASS version:

```
=animateAll($time)
  -webkit-transition: all $time ease-in-out
  -moz-transition: all $time ease-in-out
  -o-transition: all $time ease-in-out
  transition: all $time ease-in-out
```

And invoke it with:

```
+animateAll(5s)
```

Example:

SASS:

```
.animatedElement
  +animateAll(5s)
```

Compiled CSS:

```
.animatedElement {
  -webkit-transition: all 5s ease-in-out;
  -moz-transition: all 5s ease-in-out;
  -o-transition: all 5s ease-in-out;
  transition: all 5s ease-in-out;
}
```

Extending classes (@extend)

What does `@extend` make in SASS code? For example, you have a part of code that is repeating in all fonts:

```
.font-small {
  font-family: Arial;
  font-size: 12px;
  font-weight: normal;
}
```

And you don't want to repeat this part of code in the next selector. You will write in SASS:

```
.font-small-red {
  @extend .font-small;
  color: red;
}
```

The code it will generate will look like the following:

```
.font-small, .font-small-red {
    font-family: Arial;
    font-size: 12px;
    font-weight: normal;
}

.font-small-red {
    color: red;
}
```

This SASS feature is great to build optimized code. Remember to use it in your project over mixins, which will generate more code.

Importing files (@import)

In CSS, you could import CSS files into one root file with `@import`. For example:

```
@import "typography.css"
@import "grid.css"
```

In SASS, you can import SASS/SCSS files into one with an automatic merge option. In case you have, for example, two files that you want to include in one SASS file, you need to write the following code:

```
@import "typography"
@import "grid"
```

As you can see in the preceding code, you don't need to add an extension of the file into `import` as it automatically loads the SASS or SCSS file. The only thing you need to remember is to have only one file in this example named, `typography`.

Let's check how it will behave in real code. Imagine that we have two files, `_typography.sass` and `_grid.sass`.

File `_grid.sass`:

```
.grid-1of2
  float: left
  width: 50%

.grid-1of4
  float: left
  width: 25%

.grid-1of5
  float: left
  width: 20%
```

File `_typography.sass`:

```
body
  font-size: 12px

h1, h2, h3, h4, h5, h6
  font:
    family: Arial

h1
  font:
    size: 36px

h2
  font:
    size: 32px

h3
  font:
    size: 28px

h4
  font:
    size: 24px
```

```
h5
  font:
    size: 20px

h6
  font:
    size: 16px
```

Now let's create a `style.sass` file:

```
@import _typography
@import _grid
```

After compilation of `style.sass`, you will see a `style.css` file:

```
body {
    font-size: 12px;
}

h1, h2, h3, h4, h5, h6 {
    font-family: Arial;
}

h1 {
    font-size: 36px;
}

h2 {
    font-size: 32px;
}

h3 {
    font-size: 28px;
}

h4 {
    font-size: 24px;
}

h5 {
    font-size: 20px;
}

h6 {
    font-size: 16px;
}
```

```
.grid-1of2 {
    float: left;
    width: 50%;
}

.grid-1of4 {
    float: left;
    width: 25%;
}

.grid-1of5 {
    float: left;
    width: 2%;
}
```

As you can see, two files are merged into one CSS, so, additionally, we made a small optimization of code because we reduced the number of requests to the server. In case of three files, we have three requests (`style.css`, then `typography.css`, and `grid.css`). Now there will be only one request.

Using of & in SASS

Sometimes, in nesting, you will need to use the name of the selector that you are currently describing. As a best description of the problem, you need to first describe a link:

```
a {
    color: #000;
}
```

and then:

```
a:hover {
    color: #f00;
}
```

In SCSS, you can use & to do that:

```
a {
    color: #000;

    &:hover {
        color: #f00;
    }
}
```

In SASS:

```
a
  color: #000

  &:hover
    color: #f00
```

You can resolve with this element other problems like combining names:

```
.classname {}

.classname_inside {}
```

In SCSS:

```
.classname {
  &_inside {

  }
}
```

In SASS:

```
.classname
  &_inside
```

This option has been possible since SASS 3.5. It will be very helpful in creating code build in BEM methodologies.

Compass features

Compass is a very useful SASS framework, especially when you are working with a big list of icons/reusable images. What you need to do is gather all the images in one folder in your project. For example, `yourfolder/envelope.png` and `yourfloder/star.png`.

Then in your SASS code:

```
@import "compass/utilities/sprites"
@import "yourfolder/*.png"
@include all-yourfolder-sprites
```

Then in your code, you can use images as an example:

```
.simple-class-envelope
  @extend .yourfolder-envelope


.simple-class-star
  @extend .yourfolder-star
```

And it will add a code to your classes:

```
.simple-class-envelope {
  background-image: url('spriteurl.png');
  background-position: -100px -200px;
}
```

Where `-100px` and `-200px` are examples of offset in your sprite.

Simple automatization (with Gulp)

Every time we are compiling project files (for example, Compass, Jade, image optimization, and so on), we are thinking about how we can automatize and speed up the process. The first idea—some terminal snippets and compiling invokers. But we can use `grunt.js` and `gulp.js`. What are Grunt and Gulp? In short—task runners. You can define a list of tasks, which you repeat all the time, group them into some logical structure, and run.

In most projects, you can use them to automatize a process of SASS/Compass compilation.

I assume that you have installed Node.js, Ruby, SASS, and Compass. If not, I recommend you to do this first. To install all of the listed software, you need to visit:

- `https://nodejs.org/en/` to install Node.js
- `https://www.ruby-lang.org/en/` to install Ruby
- `http://sass-lang.com/` to install SASS
- `http://compass-style.org/` to install Compass
- `http://gulpjs.com/` to install Gulp globally on your machine

On these pages, you can find guides and tutorials on how to install all of this software.

Then you will need to create a basic structure for your project. It is best to create folders:

- `src`: In this folder we will keep our source files
- `dist`: In this folder we will keep our compiled files

In the `src` folder, please create a `css` folder, which will keep our SASS files.

Then in the `root` folder, run the following command line:

`npm init`

`npm install gulp-compass gulp --save-dev`

In `gulpfile.js` add the following lines of code:

```
var gulp = require('gulp'),
    compass = require('gulp-compass');

gulp.task('compass', function () {
    return gulp.src('src/styles/main.sass')
        .pipe(compass({
            sass: 'src/styles',
            image: 'src/images',
            css: 'dist/css',
            sourcemap: true,
            style: 'compressed'
        }));
});

gulp.task('default', function () {
    gulp.watch('src/css/**/*.sass', ['compass']);
});
```

Now you can run your automatizer with the following in your command line:

`gulp`

This will run the `default` task from your `gulpfile.js`, which will add a watcher to the files with `.sass` extensions, which are located in the `src/css` folder. Every time you change any file in this location, your task `compass` will run. It means that it will run the `compass` task and create a sourcemap for us. We could use a default `compass` command, but `gulp.js` is a part of the modern frontend developer workflow. We will be adding new functions to this automatizer in the next chapters.

Let's analyze the code a little deeper:

```
gulp.task('default', function () {
    gulp.watch('src/css/**/*.sass', ['compass']);
});
```

The preceding code defines the default task. It appends a watcher, which checks the `src/css/**/*.sass` location for SASS files. It means that every file in a `src/css` folder and any subsequent folder, for example, `src/css/folder/file.sass`, will have a watcher. When files in this location are changed, the task defined in the array `[compass]` will run. Our `task compass` is the only element in the array but it, of course, can be extended (we will do this in the next chapters).

Now let's analyze the `task compass`:

```
gulp.task('compass', function () {
    return gulp.src('src/styles/main.sass')
        .pipe(compass({
            sass: 'src/styles',
            image: 'src/images',
            css: 'dist/css',
            sourcemap: true,
            style: 'compressed'
        }));
});
```

It will compile the `gulp.src('src/styles/main.sass)` file and save the compiled file in `pipe (gulp.dest('style.css'))`. The `compass` task is defined in `pipe`:

```
.pipe(compass({
            sass: 'src/styles',
            image: 'src/images',
            css: 'dist/css',
            sourcemap: true,
            style: 'compressed'
        }))
```

The first line of this task defines the source folder for SASS files. The second line defines the images folder. The third line sets the destination of the CSS file. The fourth line is set to generate a source map for the file (for easier debugging).The fifth line defines the style of the saved CSS file; in this case, it will be compressed (it means that it will be ready for production code).

Pixelperfect layouts tools

In a common workflow, a graphic designer creates the design of a website/application. Then, next in the process is the HTML/CSS coding. After the development process, the project is in the **quality assurance (QA)** phase. Sometimes it's focused only on the functional side of the project, but in a good workflow, it checks of graphic design phase. During the QA process, the designer is involved, he/she will find all pixels that are not good in your code. How would check all the details in a pixelperfect project?

The question is about mobile projects. How to check if it is still pixel perfect when it needs to be flexible in browsers? You will need to make it in described ranges. For example, you have to create HTML/CSS for the web page, which has three views for mobile, tablet, and desktop. You will need plugins, which will help you to build pixel perfect layouts.

Pixelfperfect plugin

Pixelperfect plugin will help you to compare design with your HTML/CSS in your browser. This plugin is available on Firefox and Chrome. To work with it, you need to make a screenshot of your design and add it in a plugin. Then you can set a position of image and opacity. This plugin is one of the most used by frontend developers to create pixel perfect HTML layouts.

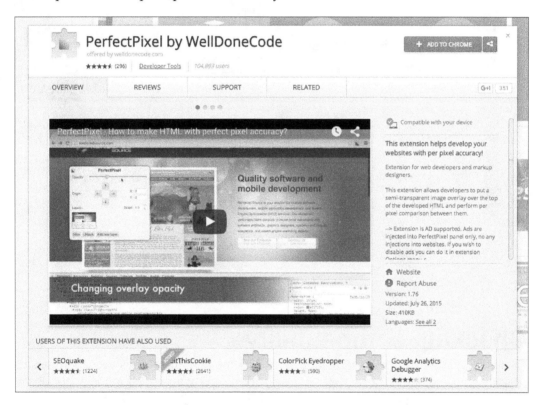

MeasureIT plugin

This plugin will help you to keep proper distances between elements, fonts, and so on. As you can see in the following screenshot, it looks like a ruler over your web page. It is easy to use—just click on the plugin icon in the browser and then click on the website (it will start the ruler), and move the cursor to the place to which you want to know the distance, and voila!

Checking compatibility

Some CSS features don't work in all browsers. Some new properties need browser-specific prefixes (like -ms, -o, -webkit) to work properly across all modern browsers. But how to check if you can use some properties in your project? Of course, you can check it yourself, but the easiest way is to check it on http://caniuse.com/. You can open this web page and check which properties you can use.

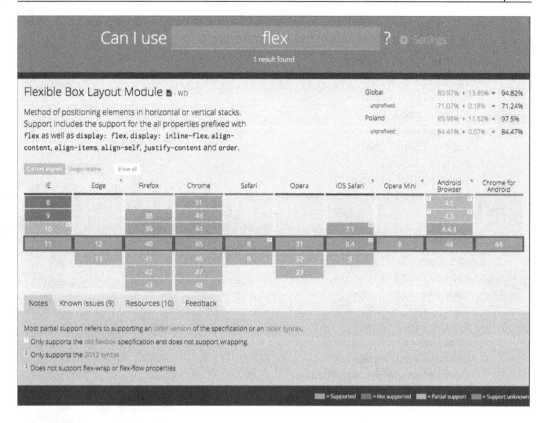

Good assumptions in code

While you are creating CSS code, you have to remember initial assumptions that will help you to keep clear and very readable code. These assumptions are as follows:

- Naming convention—You need to remember that your code needs to be the exact names of classes.

- Use comments, but not everywhere, only in places where they are needed. Yeah, but when they are needed? They are especially needed when you have some exception or when you have some quick fixes for browsers. With comments, you can describe blocks of code, which describes the views, for example, of footer/header, or any other element.

- Try to keep code which is readable and logical. But how does unlogical code look like? Look at the following two examples:

Example 1 is as follows:

```
.classname {
  font-size: 12px;
  color: red;
  font-weight: bold;
  text-align: center;
  margin: 10px;
  padding-left: 2px;
  text-transform: uppercase;
}
```

Example 2 is as follows:

```
.classname {
  margin: 10px;
  padding-left: 2px;

  font-size: 12px;
  font-weight: bold;
  text-align: center;
  text-transform: uppercase;

  color: red;
}
```

Which code looks better? Yeah, of course, the second example because it has grouped declarations. First the description of the box model, then the font and text behaviors, and finally color. You can try to keep it in another hierarchy which will be more readable for you.

Using sample 2 in SASS:

```
.classname
  margin: 10px
  padding:
    left: 2px
  font:
    size: 12px
    weight: bold
  text:
    align: center
    transform: uppercase
  color: red
```

Isn't it shorter and more logical?

- Create proper selectors (this will be described later in this chapter).
- Create an elastic structure for your files.

Creating proper selectors

The main problem of the CSS coder is creating proper selectors. Knowledge about priors in selectors is mandatory. It will help you to omit the `!important` statement in your code and will help you to create smaller and more readable files.

Using IDs

Using of IDs in CSS is rather bad behavior. The foundation of HTML says that an ID is unique and should be used only once in an HTML code. It is good to omit IDs in CSS and use them only when it is the only way to style some element:

```
#id_name {
    property: value;
}
```

Usage of IDs in CSS code is bad behavior because selectors based on ID are stronger than selectors based on classes. This is confusing in legacy code when you see that some part of the code is still preceded by another selector because it is added in the ID's parents-based selector as follows:

```
#someID .class {
    /* your code */
}
```

It is good to omit this problem in your projects. First, think twice if a selector based on an ID is a good idea in this place and if this cannot be replaced with any other "weaker" selector.

Using classes

Classes are the best friends of the HTML/CSS coder. They are reusable elements that you can define and then reuse as much as you want in your HTML code, for example:

```
.class_name {
    property: value;
}
```

Grouping selectors

You can group and nest selectors. First, let's nest them:

```
.class_wrapper .class_nested {
  property: value;
}
```

Then let's group them:

```
.class_wrapper_one,
.class_wrapper_two {
  property: value;
}
```

Interesting selectors

In CSS code, you need to be a selector specialist. It is a very important skill to make a right selector that will match a specific element in the DOM structure. Let's provide a little bit of fundamental knowledge about selectors.

Adjacent sibling combinatory +

The plus sign in CSS can be used in selectors in which you will need to select an element right after the element on the left side of the plus sign, for example:

```
p + a {
  property: value;
}
```

This selector will return a, which is right after the p selector, like in the following example:

```
<p>Text</p>
<a>Text</a>
```

But it won't work in the following case:

```
<p>Text</p>
<h1>Text</h1>
<a>Text</a>
```

Child combinator ">"

With element (>) in the selector, you can match every element that is right into the element. Let's analyze the following example:

```
p >a {
    property: value;
}
```

This selector will return all `<a>` elements which are into`<p>` element but are not nested deeper, for example:

```
<p>
<a>text</a>
</p>
```

But this won't work in the following case:

```
<p>
<span>
<a>text</a>
</span>
</p>
```

Adjacent sibling combinatory ~

With ~, you can create a selector that will match every element that is parallel in the DOM structure, for example:

```
p ~ a {
    color: pink;
}
```

This selector will work in the following cases:

```
<p></p>
<a></a>
```

and:

```
<p>Text</p>
<span>Text</span>
<a>Text</a>
```

Getting elements by attributes

Sometimes, there is no way to create a selector based on elements, classes, and IDs. So this is the moment when you need to search for any other possibility to create the right selector. It is possible to get elements by their attributes (`data`, `href`, and so on):

```
[attribute] {
    property: value;
}
```

It will return the following:

```
<p attribute>text</p>
```

And will also return the following:

```
<p attribute="1">text</p>
```

Attributes with exact value [attribute="value"]

In real CSS/HTML code, there are examples when you will need a selector which is based on attributes with an exact value like inputs with the type as text or when elements data attribute is set with some value. It is possible with a selector which is similar to this example code:

```
input[type="text"] {
    background: #0000ff;
}
```

will match:

```
<input type="text">
```

Attributes which begin with [attribute^="value"]

This selector is very useful when you want to match elements with attributes that begin with some specific string. Let's check an example:

```
<div class="container">
    <div class="grid-1of4">Grid 2</div>
    <div class="grid-1of2">Grid 1</div>
    <div class="grid-1of4">Grid 3</div>
</div>
```

SASS code:

```
.grid-1of2
width: 50%
  background: blue

.grid-1of4
width: 25%
  background: green


[class^="grid"]
  float: left
```

Compiled CSS:

```
.grid-1of2 {
    width: 50%;
    background: blue;
}

.grid-1of4 {
    width: 25%;
    background: green;
}

[class^="grid"] {
    float: left;
}
```

Let's analyze this fragment in SASS code:

```
[class^="grid"]
  float: left
```

This selector will match every element that has an attribute with a `grid` word in the beginning of this attribute. This will match in our case: `.grid-1of2` and `.grid-1of4`. Of course, we could do it with SASS:

```
.grid-1of2, .grid-1of4
float: left
```

And get it in compiled code:

```
.grid-1of2, .grid-1of4 {
    float: left;
}
```

But let's imagine that we have about 10 or maybe 40 classes like the following:

```
.grid-2of4
  width: 50%

.grid-3of4
  width: 75%

.grid-1of5
  width: 20%

.grid-2of5
  width: 40%
```

```
.grid-3of5
  width: 60%

.grid-4of5
  width: 80%
```

In compiled CSS:

```
.grid-2of4 {
    width: 50%;
}

.grid-3of4 {
    width: 75%;
}

.grid-1of5 {
    width: 20%;
}

.grid-2of5 {
    width: 40%;
}

.grid-3of5 {
    width: 60%;
}

.grid-4of5 {
    width: 80%;
}
```

And now we want to apply a `float: left` to these elements like:

```
.grid-1of2, .grid-1of4, .grid-2of4, .grid-3of4, .grid-1of5, .grid-
2of5, .grid-3of5, .grid-4of5
  float: left
```

In CSS:

```
.grid-1of2, .grid-1of4, .grid-2of4, .grid-3of4, .grid-1of5, .grid-
2of5, .grid-3of5, .grid-4of5 {
    float: left;
}
```

It is easier to use a selector based on `[attribute^="value"]` and match all of the elements with a class which starts with a grid string:

```
[class^="grid"]
  float: left
```

Whitespace separated attribute values [attribute~="value"]

With this selector you can match all elements which in list of "attributes" that contains a string described as a "value". Let's analyze the following example.

HTML:

```
<div class="container">
    <div data-style="green font10">Element green font10</div>
    <div data-style="black font24">Element black font24</div>
    <div data-style="blue font17">Element blue font17</div>
</div>
```

Now in SASS:

```
[data-style~="green"]
  color: green

[data-style~="black"]
  color: black

[data-style~="blue"]
  color: blue

[data-style~="font10"]
  font:
    size: 10px

[data-style~="font17"]
  font:
    size: 17px

[data-style~="font24"]
  font:
    size: 24px
```

Compiled CSS:

```css
[data-style~="green"] {
    color: green;
}

[data-style~="black"] {
    color: black;
}

[data-style~="blue"] {
    color: blue;
}

[data-style~="font10"] {
    font-size: 10px;
}

[data-style~="font17"] {
    font-size: 17px;
}

[data-style~="font24"] {
    font-size: 24px;
}
```

And the effect in the browser is as follows:

Element green font10
Element black font24
Element blue font17

Attribute values ending with [attribute$="value"]

In one of the previous sections, we had an example of a selector based on beginning of an attribute. But what if we need an attribute ending? With this feature comes a selector based on a pattern `[attribute$="value"]`. Let's check the following example code:

```html
<div class="container">
    <a href="/contact-form">Contact form</a><br>
    <a href="/contact">Contact page</a><br>
    <a href="/recommendation-form">Recommendation form</a>
</div>
```

SASS:

```
[href$="form"]
  color: yellowgreen
font:
    weight: bold
```

Compiled CSS:

```
[href$="form"] {
  color: yellowgreen;
  font-weight: bold;
}
```

The effect in the browser is as follows:

With the selector `[href$="form"]`, we matched all elements whose attribute `href` ends with the string `form`.

Attributes containing strings [attribute*="value"]

With this selector, you can match every element that contains a string in a value in any place. Let's analyze the following example code.

HTML:

```
<div class="container">
    <a href="/contact-form">Contact form</a><br>
    <a href="/form-contact">Contact form</a><br>
    <a href="/rocommendation-form">Recommendation form</a><br>
    <a href="/rocommendation-and-contact-form">Recommendation and
contact form</a>
</div>
```

SASS:

```
[href*="contact"]
  color: yellowgreen
  font:
    weight: bold
```

Compiled CSS:

```
[href*="contact"] {
    color: yellowgreen;
    font-weight: bold;
}
```

In the browser we will see:

Contact form
Contact form
Recommendation form
Recommendation form

With the selector `[href*="contact"]`, we matched every element that contains the `contact` string in the value of the attribute `href`.

Using !important in CSS

Hah... the magic word in CSS, which you can see in some special cases. With `!important`, you can even overwrite inline code added by JavaScript in your HTML.

How to use it? It is very simple:

```
element {
    property: value !important;
}
```

Remember to use it properly and in cases where you really need it. Don't overuse it in your code because it can have a big impact in the future, especially in cases when somebody will read your code and will try to debug it.

Preparing your project

Starting your project and planning it is one of the most important processes. You need to create a simple strategy for keeping variables and mixins and also create a proper file structure. This chapter is about the most known problems in planning your file structure and the partialization of files in your project.

Files structure

The most important thing when you are starting a project is to make a good plan of its process. First, you will need to separate settings:

- Fonts
- Variables
- Mixins

Then you will need to partialize your project. You will need to create files for repeatable elements along all sites:

- Header
- Footer
- Forms

Then you will need to prepare next partialization—specific views of styling and elements, for example:

- View home
- View blog
- View single post
- View contact page

How to keep variables in a project

What can you keep in variables? Yeah, that is a good question, for sure:

- Colors (of fonts, backgrounds, and elements)
- Global font sizes (like H1-H6, p, and so on)
- Grid dividers
- Global paddings/margins

How and where to keep mixins (local and global)

In this file, you can collect your mostly used mixins. I've divided it into local and global. In global mixins, I'm gathering the most used mixins I'm using along all projects.

In local mixins, I recommend to gather those mixins that you will use only in this project:

- Dedicated gradient
- Font styling including font family size and so on
- Hover/active states and so on

Keep typography styles in a separate file

This file is dedicated for all the most important text elements:

- `h1-h6`
- `p`
- `a`
- `strong`
- `span`

Additionally, you can add classes like the following:

- `.h1-h6`
- `.red` `.blue` (or any other which you know that will repeat in your texts)
- `.small, .large`

Why should you use classes like `.h1-.h6`?

Yeah, it's a pretty obvious question. Sometimes you cannot repeat `h1-h6` elements, but, for example, on a blog, you need to make them the same font style as `h1`. This is the best usage of this style, for example (HTML structure):

```
<h1> Main title</h1>
<h2>Subtitle</h2>
<p>... Text block ... </p>

<h2>Second subtitle</h2>
<p>... Text block ... </p>

<p class="h2">Something important</p>
<p>... Text block ... </p>

<p class="h1">Something important</p>
<p>... Text block ... </p>
```

Views of specific elements

In the following listed files, you can gather all elements that are visible in some specific views. For example, in a blog structure, you can have a view of single post or page view. So you need to create files:

```
_view_singlepost.sass
_view_singlepage.sass
_view_contactpage.sass
```

Downloading the example code

You can download the example code files for this book from your account at `http://www.packtpub.com`. If you purchased this book elsewhere, you can visit `http://www.packtpub.com/support` and register to have the files e-mailed directly to you.

You can download the code files by following these steps:

- Log in or register to our website using your e-mail address and password.
- Hover the mouse pointer on the **SUPPORT** tab at the top.
- Click on **Code Downloads & Errata**.
- Enter the name of the book in the **Search** box.
- Select the book for which you're looking to download the code files.
- Choose from the drop-down menu where you purchased this book from.
- Click on **Code Download**.

You can also download the code files by clicking on the **Code Files** button on the book's webpage at the Packt Publishing website. This page can be accessed by entering the book's name in the **Search** box. Please note that you need to be logged in to your Packt account.

Once the file is downloaded, please make sure that you unzip or extract the folder using the latest version of:

- WinRAR / 7-Zip for Windows
- Zipeg / iZip / UnRarX for Mac
- 7-Zip / PeaZip for Linux

Summary

In this chapter, you gathered information about the fundamentals of modern CSS workflow. We started with choosing an IDE and then we focused on speeding up the process through the usage of snippets, preprocessors, and processes automatization.

In the next chapter, we will focus on the basics of CSS theory, box models, positions, and displaying modes in CSS.

2
Mastering of Fundamentals

This chapter will master the box model, floating troubleshooting positioning, and display types. After this chapter, you will be more aware of the foundations of HTML and CSS.

In this chapter, we will cover the following topics:

- Gaining knowledge about the traditional box model
- Basics of floating elements
- Foundations of positioning elements on a web page
- Gaining knowledge about display types

Traditional box model

An understanding of the box model is the foundation of CSS theories. You have to know the impact of width, height, margin, and borders on the size of the box and how you can manage it to match the elements on a website. The main questions for coders and frontend developers in interviews are based on box model theories. Let's begin this important chapter, which will be the foundation for every upcoming subject.

Padding/margin/border/width/height

The ingredients of the final width and height of the box are as follows:

- Width
- Height
- Margins
- Paddings
- Borders

For better understanding of the box model, the following is an image from Google Chrome inspector:

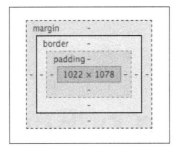

For more clarity and better understanding of the box model, let's analyze the following image:

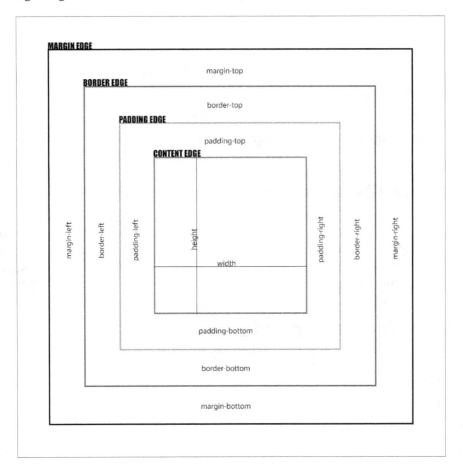

In the preceding image, you can see that in the box model, we have the following four edges:

- Content edge
- Padding edge
- Border edge
- Margin edge

The width and height of the box are based on the following:

- Width/height of content
- Padding
- Border
- Margin

The width and height of content in the box with default box-sizing are controlled by the following properties:

- Min-width
- Max-width
- Width
- Min-height
- Max-height
- Height

An important thing about the box model is how background properties will behave. The background will be included in the content section and in the padding section (to the padding edge).

Let's get a code and try to point to all elements of the box model.

HTML code:

```
<div class="element">
  Lorem ipsum dolor sit amet consecteur
</div>
```

CSS code:

```
.element {
   background: pink;
   padding: 10px;
   margin: 20px;
```

```
    width: 100px;
    height: 100px;
     border: solid 10px black;
}
```

In the browser, we will see the following:

The view from the inspector of Google Chrome is as follows:

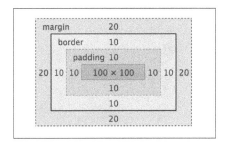

Let's check how the areas of the box model are placed in the following specific example:

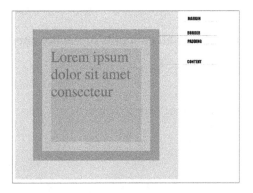

The basic task for the interviewed frontend developer is:

The box/element is described with the styles:

```
.box {
    width: 100px;
    height: 200px;
    border: 10px solid #000;
    margin: 20px;
    padding: 30px;
}
```

Please count the final `width` and `height` (the real space which is needed for this element) of this element.

So, as you can see, the problem is to count the width and height of the box.

The ingredients of width are as follows:

- Width
- Border left
- Border right
- Padding left
- Padding right

Additionally for the width of space taken by the box:

- Margin left
- Margin right

The ingredients of height are as follows:

- Height
- Border top
- Border bottom
- Padding top
- Padding bottom

Additionally for height of space taken by the box:

- Margin top
- Margin bottom

Therefore, when you sum the elements, you will have the following equations:

Width:

```
Box width = width + borderLeft + borderRight + paddingLeft +
paddingRight
Box width = 100px + 10px + 10px + 30px + 30px = 180px
```

Space width:

```
width = width + borderLeft + borderRight + paddingLeft + paddingRight
+  marginLeft + marginRight
width = 100px + 10px + 10px + 30px + 30px + 20px + 20 px = 220px
```

Height:

```
Box height = height + borderTop + borderBottom + paddingTop +
paddingBottom
Box height  = 200px + 10px + 10px + 30px + 30px = 280px
```

Space height:

```
Space height = height + borderTop + borderBottom + paddingTop +
paddingBottom +  marginTop + marginBottom
Space height = 200px + 10px + 10px + 30px + 30px + 20px + 20px = 320px
```

You can check it in the real browser as shown in the following:

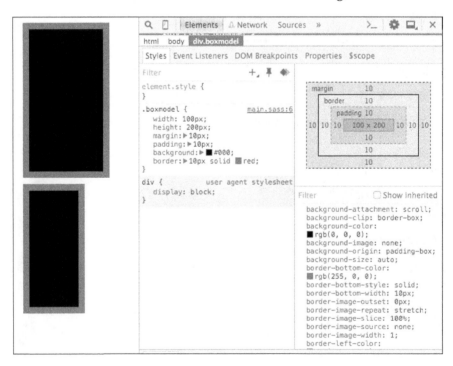

Omitting problems with the traditional box model (box-sizing)

Basic theory of the box model is pretty hard to learn. You need to remember all the elements of width/height, even if you set the width and height. The hardest thing for beginners to understand is padding, which shouldn't be counted as a component of width and height. It should be *inside* the box and it should impact on this value. To change these behaviors with CSS3, supported since Internet Explorer 8, comes box-sizing.

You can set the value as follows:

```
box-sizing: border-box
```

What does it give to you? Finally, the counting of box width and height will be easier because box padding and the border are inside the box. So if we are taking our previous class:

```
.box {
    width: 100px;
    height: 200px;
    border: 10px solid #000;
    margin: 20px;
    padding: 30px;
}
```

We can count the width and height easily:

```
Width = 100px
Height = 200px
```

Additionally, the space taken by the box:

- Space width = 140px (because the 20px margin is on both sides left and right)
- Space height = 240px (because the 20px margin is on both sides top and bottom)

The following is a sample from Google Chrome:

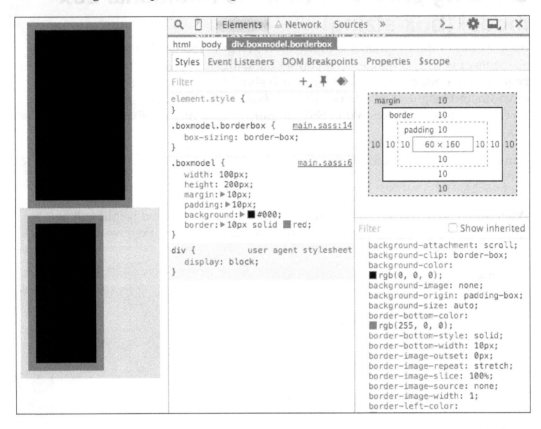

Therefore, if you do not want to repeat all the problems of the traditional box model, you should use it globally for all elements. Of course, it's not recommended for old projects, for example, a new client who needs some small changes in the old project. If you add the following code:

```
* {
width: 100px;
}
```

You can cause more harm than good because of the inheritance of this property for all elements, which are now based on the traditional box model. But for all new projects, you should use it.

Floating elements

Floating boxes are the most used in modern layouts. The theory of floating boxes was used especially in grid systems and inline lists in CSS frameworks. For example, class and mixin inline lists (in the Zurb Foundation framework) are based on floats.

Possibilities of floating elements

Elements can be floated to the left and right side. Of course, there is a method to reset floats too. The possible values are as follows:

```
float: left; // will float element to left
float: right; // will float element to right
float: none; // will reset float
```

Most known floating problems

When you are using floating elements, you can have some issues. The most known problems with floated elements are as follows:

- Too big elements (because of width, margin left/right, padding left/right, and badly counted width, which is based on the box model)
- Not cleared floats

All of these problems provide specific effects, which you can easily recognize and then fix.

Elements which are too big can be recognized when they are not in one line, as they should be. What you should check first is if the box-sizing: border-box is applied, and then check width, padding, and margin.

You can easily recognize floats that are not cleared when the floating structure of some elements from next container are *floated*. This means that you have no clear fix in your floating container.

Defining clear fix/class/mixins

When I started developing HTML and CSS code, there was a method to clear the floats with .cb or .clear classes, both of which were defined as follows:

```
.clearboth, .cb {
    clear: both
}
```

This element was added in a container right after all the floated elements. This is important to remember about clearing the floats because containers that contains floating elements won't inherit the height of the highest floating element (which will have a height equal to 0),for example:

```
<div class="container">
    <div class="float">
        … content ...
    </div>
    <div class="float">
        … content ...
    </div>
    <div class="clearboth"></div>
</div>
```

CSS looks like the following:

```
.float {
    width: 100px;
    height: 100px;
    float: left;
}

.clearboth {
    clear: both
}
```

Nowadays, there is a better and faster way to clear floats. You can do this with the clear fix element, which can be defined as follows:

```
.clearfix:after {
    content: "";
    visibility: hidden;
    display: block;
    height: 0;
    clear: both;
}
```

And you can use it in HTML code:

```
<div class="container clearfix">
    <div class="float">
        ... content ...
    </div>
    <div class="float">
        ... content ...
    </div>
</div>

</div>
```

The main reason to switch on `clear fix` is that you save one tag (with the `clearboth` class). Recommended usage is based on the `clear fix` mixin, which you can define in SASS as follows:

```
=clear fix
&:after
    content: ""
    visibility: hidden
    display: block
    height: 0
    clear: both
```

Therefore, every time you need to clear floating in some container, you need to invoke it. For example, let us take the previous code:

```
<div class="container">
<div class="float">
        … content ...
</div>
<div class="float">
        … content ...
</div>
</div>
```

The container can be described as follows:

```
.container
  +clear fix
```

Example of using floating elements

The most known usage of float elements is grids. A grid is mainly used to structure the data displayed on a web page. In this chapter, let's check just a short draft of a grid. In the upcoming chapters, we will focus on automatization of creating the grid with mixins.

Let us create some HTML code:

```
<div class="row">
    <div class="column_1of2">
        Lorem
    </div>
    <div class="column_1of2">
        Lorem
    </div>
```

```
    </div>
    <div class="row">
        <div class="column_1of3">
            Lorem
        </div>
        <div class="column_1of3">
            Lorem
        </div>
        <div class="column_1of3">
            Lorem
        </div>

    </div>

    <div class="row">
        <div class="column_1of4">
            Lorem
        </div>
        <div class="column_1of4">
            Lorem
        </div>
        <div class="column_1of4">
            Lorem
        </div>
        <div class="column_1of4">
            Lorem
        </div>
    </div>
```

And also create some SASS code:

```
*
  box-sizing: border-box

=clear fix
&:after
    content: ""
    visibility: hidden
    display: block
    height: 0
    clear: both

.row
  +clear fix
```

```
.column_1of2
  background: orange
  width: 50%
  float: left


&:nth-child(2n)
    background: red


.column_1of3
  background: orange
  width: (100% / 3)
  float: left


&:nth-child(2n)
    background: red


.column_1of4
  background: orange
  width: 25%
  float: left


&:nth-child(2n)
    background: red
```

The final effect is as follows:

As you can see, we created a structure of a basic grid. In places where HTML code is placed Lorem here is a full lorem ipsum to illustrate the grid system.

Display types

There are a few display types in CSS whose definition and behaviors are the foundation of frontend developers. The most known and basic display values are as follows:

- Inline
- Block
- Inline-block
- Table/table-cell
- Flex (this will be described further in this book)

Block elements

Block elements always start from a new line. The most important properties of block elements are width and height, which can be changed from CSS code. For better understanding, let's check the following screenshot:

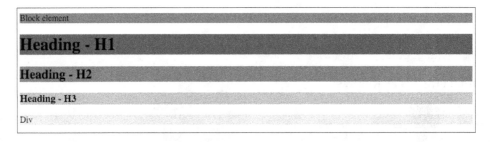

It is easy to see that all the block elements are taking as much width as they can.

The mainly used HTML block-level elements are as follows:

- address
- article
- aside
- blockquote
- canvas
- div
- footer
- form
- h1, h2, h3, h4, h5, h6

- header
- main
- nav
- ol
- output
- p
- pre
- section
- table
- ul
- video

Inline elements

Inline elements can be described as elements that take as much space as they need. It can be best described using the following image:

The mainly used HTML inline-level elements are as follows:

- acronym
- cite
- code
- dfn
- strong
- samp
- var
- a
- bdo
- br
- img
- map

- object
- script
- span
- sub
- sup
- button
- input
- label
- select
- textarea

Inline-block display

Inline elements are elements that gather properties of inline and block elements. Inline elements take as much space as they need, but additionally you can set their width, height, and padding. On the following image which is added (after the code listings), you can see the following code:

```html
<body>
<p> Block element </p>
<span>Inline element</span>
<p class="width300"> Block element width 300 </p>
<span class="width300">Inline element width 300</span>
<span class="width300 dib"> Block element width 300 </span>
</body>
```

Described with SASS code:

```sass
p, span
  background: red

&.width300
    width: 300px

.dib
  display: inline-block
```

Compiled to CSS:

```css
p, span {
  background: red;
}
p.width300,
span.width300 {
```

```
      width: 300px;
  }

  .dib {
    display: inline-block;
  }
```

Block element

Inline element

Block element width 300

Inline element width 300 Block element width 300

As you can easily see, the first element is a block element and it takes as much width as it can. The second element is inline. The third is a block element with a set width (300 pixels). The fourth element is inline with a set width (300 pixels) but it is not applied to this element because it has no proper display type. In addition, the last element is a span whose normal display type is inline but is set in CSS to inline block. After this operation, you can set the width of the element, and, additionally, it naturally floats to the previous inline element.

Where can you use other types of elements – navigation

The most known problem related to types of display is inline navigations. For better understanding, let's create a markup as follows:

```
<nav class="main-navigation">
    <ul>
        <li>
            <a href="#">First element</a>
        </li>
        <li>
            <a href="#">Second element</a>
        </li>
        <li>
            <a href="#"> Third element</a>
        </li>
    </ul>
</nav>
```

The easiest way to make the elements in one line is to use `float:left`, for example:

```
.main-navigation
  ul
    +clear fix /* This will prevent problems of cleared float */
    list-style: none

  li
    float: left
```

The second idea is to use `display: inline-block` on the `li` element:

```
.main-navigation
  ul
    list-style: none

  li
    display: inline-block
```

Where can you use other types of elements – problem of equal boxes

There is a one problem, which is repeating on web pages, and you will need to append some JavaScript code to apply the same height. It was necessary to do that back in the days. Firstly, the heights of boxes were measured and then the bigger height was set as the height, which would be applied to another box. Finally, the height would be applied to all equalized boxes.

Nowadays, you can use a table-cell value of display.

HTML code:

```
<div class="equalizer">
    <div class="equalized">
        Lorem ipsum dolor sit amet, consectetur adipisicing elit.
    </div>
    <div class="equalized">
        Lorem ipsum dolor sit amet, consectetur adipisicing elit.
    </div>
    <div class="equalized">
        Lorem ipsum dolor sit amet, consectetur adipisicing elit.
Nam, soluta voluptatem accusamus totam possimus corporis inventore
consequuntur unde ut deserunt reiciendis quis aspernatur, ea quisquam
numquam veniam illo, cum culpa.
    </div>
</div>
```

SASS code:

```
.equalizer
  display: table
  background: orange

.equalized
  display: table-cell
  width: 300px
  background: yellow
```

The effect in the browser is as shown in the following:

Lorem ipsum dolor sit amet, consectetur adipisicing elit.	Lorem ipsum dolor sit amet, consectetur adipisicing elit.	Lorem ipsum dolor sit amet, consectetur adipisicing elit. Nam, soluta voluptatem accusamus totam possimus corporis inventore consequuntur unde ut deserunt reiciendis quis aspernatur, ea quisquam numquam veniam illo, cum culpa.

CSS elements positioning

Understanding of positions in CSS is one of the key skills of frontend developers. It helps you to change the behavior of each element on a web page. Additionally, with a mix of positions, you can change the behavior of the inner (child) elements.

Static, relative, absolute, fixed – differences

The position static is a default value of the position, which includes every element on a web page.

The position relative is making an element relative to itself. You can easily understand it with the following code:

```
<p>
    Lorem
    <span> ipsum</span>
</p>
```

And create the SASS:

```
span
  position: relative
  top: -10px
```

What you should see before appending the styles is as shown in the following:

> Lorem ipsum dolor sit amet

In addition, after appending the styles you will see the following:

> Lorem ^{ipsum} dolor sit amet

As you can see, when we change the position to `relative` and move it with property top, left, right, or bottom, we will move the element from its current position.

Additionally, relatively positioned elements can be set as a scope for inner elements with the position absolute, for example, HTML:

```
<div class="relative">
    <div class="absolute"></div>
</div>
```

SASS:

```
.relative
  width: 200px
  height: 200px
  background: orange
  position: relative

.absolute
  width: 40px
  height: 40px
  background: red
  position: absolute
  left: 100px
  top: 30px
```

The effect in the browser is as shown in the following:

The orange box is a `.relative` element. The smaller box is absolutely positioned and related with the `relative` element.

The position `absolute` can be used as in the preceding example. But what will happen when there isn't a parent relative element? Absolutely positioned elements will be related with HTML DOM elements.

Fixed elements are strictly fixed to the browser. So when you apply position: `fixed` to any element and give it top: 0 and left: 0, this element will be stuck to the top-left corner of the browser. Even when the scroll action is done, the element won't change its position related to the browser.

The following code will show you how fixed elements are behaving.

HTML:

```
<body>
<div class="fixed">
    position: fixed
</div>

<ul>
    <li>Lorem</li>
    <li>Ipsum</li>
    <li>Dolor</li>
    <li>Sit</li>
    <li>Amet</li>
</ul>
</body>
```

SASS:

```
body
    padding-top: 100px
    background: red

.fixed
    position: fixed
    text-align: center
    top: 0
    left: 0
    height: 100px
    width: 100%
    background: blue


ul
    height: 2000px
```

As you can see in the preceding code, the `body` element has `padding-top`, which is equal to the height of the `.fixed` element. This is caused by the `fixed` element that normally when you remove the padding `fixed` element will be over the `body` content (it will cover this element). The following screenshot shows the browser before the scroll action and the next screenshot shows the browser after the scroll action. Both screenshots contain the border of the browser to show the proper scroll action.

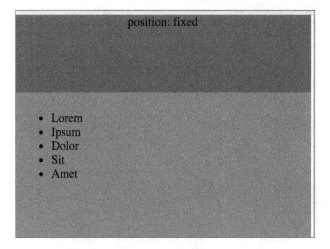

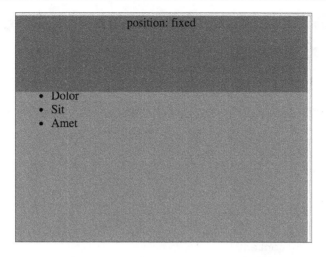

Important properties, which you can add to elements with positions, `relative/fixed/absolute`, are as follows:

- Left
- Right
- Top
- Bottom
- Z-index

A common problem during the coding of the position is overriding the `left` value by applying the `right` value. A sample code is as follows:

```
.element
  position: absolute
  left: 10px
  right: 20px
```

The `.element` will be still stuck to its left position. How do you append it to the right position?

```
.element
  position: absolute
  left: auto
  right: 20px
```

Lists with fixed images (on the right or left) and descriptions

This is a pretty common problem relating to lists. Lists of articles with fixed images (with fixed width and height) on the one side and with elastic content on the right could be pretty problematic without the positions `relative` and `absolute`. Following is an example.

HTML:

```
<article>
    <div class="image">
        <img src="image.jpg"/>
    </div>
    <div class="content">
        <p class="header">Header</p>
        <p class="description">Lorem ipsum dolor sit amet, consectetur
adipiscing elit, sed do eiusmod tempor incididunt ut labore et dolore
magna aliqua</p>
    </div>
</article>
```

SASS:

```
*
  box-sizing: border-box

article
  position: relative
  padding: 10px
    left: 220px
  height: 220px
  background: red

  .image
    position: absolute
    left: 10px
    top: 10px
    background: #000
    width: 200px
    height: 200px

  .content
    width: 100%
```

CSS code after compilation:

```css
* {
    box-sizing: border-box;
}

article {
    position: relative;
    padding: 10px;
    padding-left: 220px;
    height: 220px;
    background: red;
}

article .image {
    position: absolute;
    left: 10px;
    top: 10px;
    background: #000;
    width: 200px;
    height: 200px;
}

article .content {
    width: 100%;
}
```

The effect in the browser is as shown in the following:

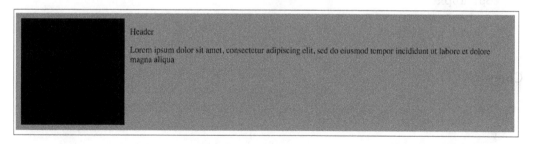

The effect after resize of the browser is as shown in the following:

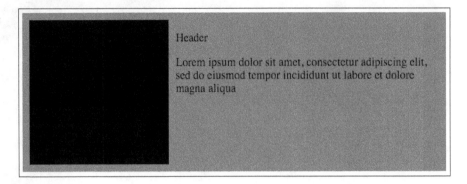

When you want to get the image on the right side, you will need to make the following changes:

```
article
  position: relative
  padding: 10px
    right: 220px // change here
height: 220px
  background: red


  .image
    position: absolute
    right: 10px // change here
top: 10px
    background: #000
    width: 200px
    height: 200px
```

Compiled CSS:

```
* {
    box-sizing: border-box;
}

article {
    position: relative;
    padding: 10px;
    padding-right: 220px;
    height: 220px;
    background: red;
```

```
}

article .image {
    position: absolute;
    right: 10px;
    top: 10px;
    background: #000;
    width: 200px;
    height: 200px;
}
```

The effect in the browser is as shown in the following:

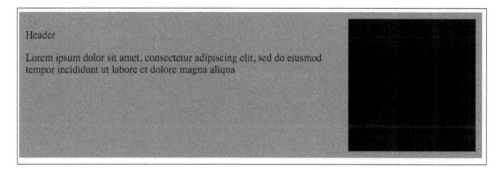

Summary

This chapter builds strong fundamentals for professional usage of CSS. You gathered the knowledge about the box model, positions, and floating elements. The next chapter is going to be a story about pseudoclasses.

3
Mastering of Pseudoelements and Pseudoclasses

Adding simple interactions on websites using CSS is known since pseudoclasses are available. Knowledge about how this feature can be used on websites is very important. Pseudoelements can be used in browsers such as Internet Explorer 8/9 + and can help with some repeatable elements on web pages that were in most cases added with empty `spans` and `divs`, for example, graphical details such as arrows in buttons, triangles, and so on. With pseudoelements, you can add these elements without creating DOM elements.

Drawing primitives is a very important skill, especially when you link them with pseudoelements into which you can add them. Adding triangles or some other specific elements can be a very important feature as you don't have to cut these graphical elements as a background or `img` element.

This chapter will master pseudoelements, pseudoclasses, and the drawing of primitives in CSS code. Finally, in each section, you can combine these elements into practical and reusable code.

In this chapter, we will:

- Learn the use of pseudoclasses
- Learn the use of pseudoelements
- Learn how to draw primitives
- Create a lot of reusable mixins in SASS

Pseudoclasses

Pseudoclasses are used in CSS to describe elements, behavior after specific actions. Actions supported by pseudoclasses are as follows:

- Mouse hover
- Mouse click/touch
- Input focus

Another use of pseudoclasses is matching elements in a specific container described by the order in this container:

- First child, last child
- Any child
- Any child of type

The most important feature of pseudoclasses you can see on links (`<a>` elements with `href` attribute).

How can we check :active, :hover state?

Hover state can be checked whenever you move your mouse pointer over the link. The easiest use of this property can be checked with the following code:

HTML:

```
<a href="#"> Title of link</a>
```

SASS:

```
a
  color: #000
  background: #fff


a:hover
  color: #fff
  background: #000
```

Generated CSS code:

```
a {
    color: #000;
    background: #fff;
}
```

```
a:hover {
    color: #fff;
    background: #000;
}
```

With the preceding code, whenever you hover the mouse over the link, the color and background of the link will be changed.

Usage – multilevel menu

A multilevel menu is the most use of action of hover state. Drop-down menus can be developed with simple HTML and CSS. You can see it on almost every website. Understanding how to build it can be the foundation for more complex solutions. Let's build a multilevel navigation and base it on the following:

HTML code:

```
<ul>
    <li>
        <a href="#">Level one - item one</a>
        <ul>
            <li><a href="#">Level two - item one</a></li>
            <li><a href="#">Level two - item two</a></li>
            <li><a href="#">Level two - item three</a></li>
            <li><a href="#">Level two - item four</a></li>
        </ul>
    </li>
    <li>
        <a href="#">Level two - item one</a>
        <ul>
            <li><a href="#">Level two - item one</a></li>
            <li><a href="#">Level two - item two</a></li>
            <li><a href="#">Level two - item three</a></li>
            <li><a href="#">Level two - item four</a></li>
        </ul>
    </li>
    <li>
        <a href="#">Level one - item three</a>
        <ul>
            <li><a href="#">Level three - item one</a></li>
            <li><a href="#">Level three - item two</a></li>
            <li><a href="#">Level three - item three</a></li>
            <li><a href="#">Level three - item four</a></li>
        </ul>
    </li>
    <ul>
```

SASS code:

```
ul
  list-style: none
  padding: 0

ul > li
  float: left
  display: inline-block
  position: relative
  margin-right: 10px

  &:hover
    ul
      display: block
      width: 200px


ul ul
  display: none
  position: absolute
  left: 0


  li
    display: block
```

Compiled CSS:

```
ul {
    list-style: none;
    padding: 0;
}

ul >li {
    float: left;
    display: inline-block;
    position: relative;
    margin-right: 10px;
}

ul >li:hover ul {
    display: block;
```

```
    width: 200px;
}

ul ul {
    display: none;
    position: absolute;
    left: 0;
}

ul ul li {
    display: block;
}
```

The effect without hover on any element can be seen in the following screenshot:

Level one - item one   Level two - item one   Level one - item three

After hovering on the second element:

Level one - item one   Level two - item one   Level one - item three
                        Level two - item one
                        Level two - item two
                        Level two - item three
                        Level two - item four

Usage – CSS hover rows

In short HTML tables, it's easy to read all the content. But in cases where you have a
lot of data (especially on financial websites) allocated in a lot of rows and columns, it's
easy to make the table unreadable. There are a few methods to simplify the reading
process. The easiest way is to add a hover action for all rows. Every time you point to a
row, it will change the background color. Let's use the following HTML code:

```
<table>
    <thead>
    <tr>
        <th> Col one header</th>
        <th> Col two header</th>
        <th> Col three header</th>
    </tr>
    </thead>
    <tbody>
```

```
    <tr>
        <td> Col one header</td>
        <td> Col two header</td>
        <td> Col three header</td>
    </tr>
    <tr>
        <td> Col one header</td>
        <td> Col two header</td>
        <td> Col three header</td>
    </tr>
    <tr>
        <td> Col one header</td>
        <td> Col two header</td>
        <td> Col three header</td>
    </tr>
    <tr>
        <td> Col one header</td>
        <td> Col two header</td>
        <td> Col three header</td>
    </tr>
    </tbody>
</table>
```

Let's assume that the count of rows (`tr` elements in `tbody`) is almost infinite. This can bring us a really long table. For ease of readability, we can add a hover action for each row as follows:

SASS:

```
tbody
  tr:hover
    background: #d3d3d3
```

Compiled CSS:

```
tbody tr:hover {
    background: #d3d3d3;
}
```

Every time you hover over each row, you can see the effect as shown in the following screenshot (the gray row is hovered over):

Col one header	**Col two header**	**Col three header**
Col one header	Col two header	Col three header
Col one header	Col two header	Col three header
Col one header	Col two header	Col three header
Col one header	Col two header	Col three header

Usage of pseudoclasses

New pseudoclasses are opening new horizons for CSS/HTML coders. Most of the features like `first-child`, `last-child`, and `nth-child`, were added with JavaScript code. For example, using jQuery code, you could get a list element and add specific classes to the first/last/nth element, and then to properly create a selector, you could add a CSS code.

But when it is natively supported by a browser, it is better to use CSS. Let's gather basic knowledge about this feature.

How to use :first-child, :last-child, :nth-child()

A short introduction to these pseudoelements is as follows:

- `:first-child`: This points to the element that is the first child of its parent
- `:last-child`: This points to the element that is the last child of its parent
- `:nth-child()`: This points to the element that matches the pattern wrapped in `()`

The easiest way to check how it works is to create an unordered list with new elements:

```
<ul>
    <li>Element one</li>
    <li>Element two</li>
    <li>Element three</li>
    <li>Element four</li>
    <li>Element five</li>
    <li>Element six</li>
    <li>Element seven</li>
    <li>Element eight</li>
</ul>
```

Let's assume that we need to stylize elements of the list. The first style we need to add is only related to the first element of the list. The easiest way to do that is to add a specific class to this element as follows:

```
<li class="first_element>Element one</li>
```

Then add a specific CSS/SASS code for it:

SASS code:

```
.first_element
  color: #f00
```

Compiled CSS:

```
.first_element {
    color: #f00;
}
```

With usage of new pseudoclasses:

```
li:first-child
  color: #00f
```

Or:

```
li:nth-child(1)
  color: #00f
```

Compiled to:

```
li:first-child {
    color: #00f;
}

li:nth-child(1) {
    color: #00f;
}
```

The second style we need to append is to make the blue text color for the last element. Easiest way is to change the HTML code:

```
<li class="last_element">Element eight</li>
```

And then add a specific CSS/SASS code for it:

```
.last_element
  color: #00f
```

Compiled to:

```
.last_element {
  color: #00f;
}
```

With the use of new pseudoclasses:

```
li:last-child
  color: #00f
```

Compiled to:

```
li:last-child {
  color: #00f;
}
```

In this case, we don't care about the count of the elements in the list. The last element of the list will always have the preceding CSS code.

Add a styling for the eighth element as follows:

```
li:nth-child(8)
  color: #00f
```

Compiled:

```
li:nth-child(8) {
  color: #00f;
}
```

In this case, we care about the count elements. The eighth element of the list will always have the preceding CSS code.

Let's assume that we want to make the fifth element orange. The easiest way to do that is to change the HTML code:

```
<li class="fifth_element">Element five</li>
```

And then append the CSS code:

```
.fifth_element
  color: orange
```

With pseudoclasses, we can draw SASS like this:

```
li:nth-child(5)
  color: orange
```

Code in browser:

- Element one
- Element two
- Element three
- Element four
- Element five
- Element six
- Element seven
- Element eight

Usage – styling table

Practical examples are best for learning. The most repeatable case where we can use all properties of pseudoclasses is tables. Let's get the following HTML code:

```
<table>
    <thead>
    <tr>
        <th> Col one header</th>
        <th> Col two header</th>
        <th> Col three header</th>
    </tr>
    </thead>
    <tbody>
    <tr>
        <td> Col one content</td>
        <td> Col two content</td>
        <td> Col three content</td>
    </tr>
    <tr>
        <td> Col one content</td>
        <td> Col two content</td>
        <td> Col three content</td>
    </tr>
    <tr>
        <td> Col one content</td>
        <td> Col two content</td>
        <td> Col three content</td>
    </tr>
    <tr>
        <td> Col one content</td>
        <td> Col two content</td>
```

```
        <td> Col three content</td>
    </tr>
    </tbody>
</table>
```

Let's make zebra styling for the table; this makes reading a table easier:

```
tbody
  tr:nth-child(2n)
    background: #d3d3d3
```

Compiled CSS:

```
tbody tr:nth-child(2n) {
    background: #d3d3d3;
}
```

This style will add a gray background to every second element in the table, as shown in the following screenshot:

Exploring :nth-child parameters

As a parameter of the :nth-child based selector, you can use any of the following:

- **Even**: This will match all even elements
- **Odd**: This will match all odd elements

Additionally, you can use an *an+b* parameter, for example:

- **3n+1**: This will match elements with indexes (counting from 1): 1, 4, 7, 10,...
- **–n+5**: This will match elements from 1 to 5
- **2n+4**: This will match elements: 4, 6, 8, 10, 12, ...

How to use :nth-last-child

This pseudoclass works similar to `nth-child`. The difference is that `nth-child` is getting the start of its work at the beginning of the list and `nth-last-child` is starting at the end of the list:

- **Even**: This will match all even elements starting at the last element
- **Odd**: This will match all odd elements starting at the last element

You can use an *an+b* parameter, as we used in `nth-child`:

- **3n+1**: This will match elements with indexes (counting from last element): 1, 4, 7, 10, …
- **–n+5**: This will match the last five elements
- **2n+4**: This will match elements: 4, 6, 8, 10, 12, … (counting from the last element)

How to use :first-of-type, :last-of-type, :nth-of-type, and :nth-last-of-type

These pseudoclasses are related to elements in the container in which are gathered a few elements. It works similar to the nth-child mechanism. For better understanding, let's begin with the following HTML code:

```
<div class="parent">
    <span>First span</span><br/>
    <strong>First strong</strong><br/>
    <span>Second span</span><br/>
    <strong>Second strong</strong><br/>
    <span>Third span</span><br/>
    <strong>Third strong</strong><br/>
    <span>Fourth span</span><br/>
    <strong>Fourth strong</strong><br/>
    <span>Fifth span</span>
</div>
```

SASS code:

```
.parent
  span
    &:first-of-type
```

```
    color: red

  &:last-of-type
    color: red

 strong
   &:nth-of-type(2)
     color: pink

   &:nth-last-of-type(2)
     color: magenta
```

Compiled to CSS:

```
.parent span:first-of-type {
    color: red;
}

.parent span:last-of-type {
    color: red;
}

.parent strong:nth-of-type(2) {
    color: pink;
}

.parent strong:nth-last-of-type(2) {
    color: magenta;
}
```

Let's bring some explanation:

- **.parent span:first-of-type**: This will match the first element in `.parent div` (`<div class="parent">`), which is span

- **.parent span:last-of-type**: This will match the last element in `.parent`, which is span

- **.parent strong:nth-of-type(2)**: This will match the second element, which is strong

- **.parent strong:nth-last-of-type(2)**: This will match the second element counting from the last element, *which is strong* as shown in the following screenshot:

First span
First strong
Second span
Second strong
Third span
Third strong
Fourth span
Fourth strong
Fifth span

Empty elements with the :empty pseudoclass

Sometimes you will need to deal with lists in which you need to treat empty elements with one CSS block of code and elements with content with another block of code. The easiest way is to add an *empty* class to its elements and you can do it without interference in the HTML code. Let's get the HTML code:

```
<ul>
    <li class="box">Black text</li>
    <li class="box"></li>
    <li class="box">Black text</li>
    <li class="box"></li>
    <li class="box"></li>
    <li class="box">Black text</li>
    <li class="box"></li>
</ul>
```

And SASS code:

```
ul
    list-style: none

.box
    background: white
    color: black
    text-align: center
    height: 100px
    width: 100px
```

```
    float: left

  .box:empty
    color: black
    background: black
```

Compiled to CSS:

```
ul {
    list-style: none;
}

.box {
    background: white;
    color: black;
    text-align: center;
    height: 100px;
    width: 100px;
    float: left;
}

.box:empty {
    color: black;
    background: black;
}
```

This will show us the following view in the browser:

It's easily to analyze the preceding code. All empty elements (which have no child) have a black background. All elements with children have a white background and black text.

Supporting forms styling with pseudoclasses

You can support the validation and simple interaction of forms with CSS code. In the following sections, you will see how to use CSS selectors for simple validation and simple interactions of inputs. With proper CSS code, you can also check if any element is required or disabled. Let's see how this is done.

Validation with :valid and :invalid

Earlier validation was done with JavaScript code. With proper CSS code, you can do it only with good selectors. Let's check it with the HTML and CSS code:

HTML code:

```html
<form class="simple_validation">
    <input type="number" min="5" max="10" placeholder="Number">
    <input type="email" placeholder="Email">
    <input type="text" required placeholder="Your name"/>
</form>
```

SASS code:

```sass
.simple_validation
  padding: 10px
  width: 400px
  box-sizing: border-box

  &:valid
    background: lightgreen

  &:invalid
    background: lightcoral

  input
    display: block
    margin: 10px 0
    width: 100%
    box-sizing: border-box

    &:valid
      border: 3px solid green

    &:invalid
      border: 3px solid red
```

Compiled CSS:

```css
.simple_validation {
    padding: 10px;
    width: 400px;
    box-sizing: border-box;
}

.simple_validation:valid {
    background: lightgreen;
}

.simple_validation:invalid {
    background: lightcoral;
}

.simple_validation input {
    display: block;
    margin: 10px 0;
    width: 100%;
    box-sizing: border-box;
}

.simple_validation input:valid {
    border: 3px solid green;
}

.simple_validation input:invalid {
    border: 3px solid red;
}
```

In the preceding example, you can check how valid and invalid pseudoclasses work. Every time you input e-mail into e-mail string, which is not e-mail address, the input will have a red border and the background of the form will change its color to light red (lightcoral). It's the same in the case of an input with number, which needs to be in the range from 5 to 10. Additionally, to input with type text, there is added attribute required. If there is no input, it has an :invalid pseudoclass.

Adding input statuses :focus, :checked, :disabled

Focus pseudoclasses are related to inputs that currently receive focus. Remember that this can be done by the user with a mouse pointer and a keyboard with the *Tab* key. Pseudoclass checked is related to inputs type checkbox and radio and matches the elements which state is changed to checked. To show how it exactly works, let's modify the HTML code we used in the previous section:

HTML code:

```
<form class="simple_validation">
    <input type="number" min="5" max="10" placeholder="Number">
    <input type="email" placeholder="Email">
    <input type="text" required placeholder="Your name"/>

    <input type="checkbox" id="newsletter"></input>
    <label for="newsletter">checked</label>
</form>
```

SASS code:

```
.simple_validation
  padding: 10px
  width: 400px
  box-sizing: border-box

  &:valid
    background: lightgreen

  &:invalid
    background: lightcoral

  label
    display: inline-block

    &:before
      content: 'Not '

  input
    display: block
    margin: 10px 0
    width: 100%
```

```
        box-sizing: border-box

        &:valid
          border: 3px solid green

        &:invalid
          border: 3px solid red

        &:focus
          background: orange
          color: red
          border: 3px solid orange

        &[type="checkbox"]
          display: inline-block
          width: 20px

          &:checked
            & + label
              color: red

              &:before
                content: 'Is '
```

Compiled CSS:

```
.simple_validation {
    padding: 10px;
    width: 400px;
    box-sizing: border-box;
}

.simple_validation:valid {
    background: lightgreen;
}

.simple_validation:invalid {
    background: lightcoral;
}

.simple_validation label {
    display: inline-block;
}

.simple_validation label:before {
```

```css
    content: "Not ";
}

.simple_validation input {
    display: block;
    margin: 10px 0;
    width: 100%;
    box-sizing: border-box;
}

.simple_validation input:valid {
    border: 3px solid green;
}

.simple_validation input:invalid {
    border: 3px solid red;
}

.simple_validation input:focus {
    background: orange;
    color: red;
    border: 3px solid orange;
}

.simple_validation input[type="checkbox"] {
    display: inline-block;
    width: 20px;
}

.simple_validation input[type="checkbox"]:checked + label {
    color: red;
}

.simple_validation input[type="checkbox"]:checked + label:before {
    content: "Is ";
}
```

The preceding example adds more interactivity to the form. The first new feature is the changing color of the focused element to red and its background/border to orange. The second feature is the interaction related to the checkbox. After changing its status to checked, it changes the `:before` element (this will be better described in the next section). At init, the `:before` element is set to `"Not "`. With HTML code gives fully `"Not checked"`. After the checkbox is checked, the `before` element is changed to `"Is "` and shows the full string equal to `"Is checked"`.

Let's check how it will look in the browser. The following screenshot appears at the start of the page:

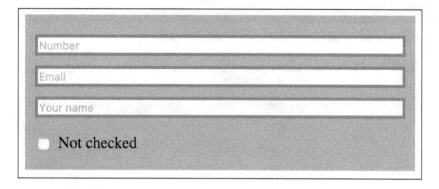

The following one will appear when the checkbox is checked:

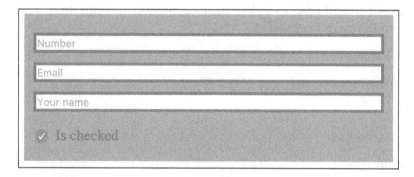

There is a visible change of the label's before element, as shown in the following screenshot, which also shows the focus of input:

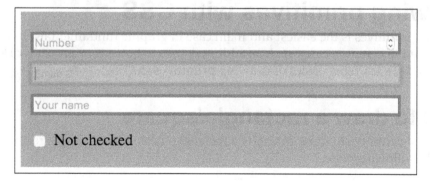

The validated form is as follows:

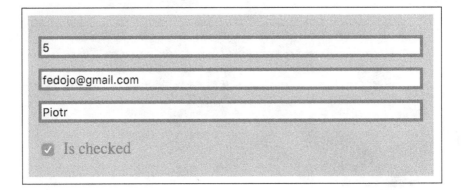

Additional aspect – colorize the placeholder

Yes, of course! You will need to stylize the placeholder. You can do it but this property is additionally prefixed:

For Internet Explorer:

```
:-ms-input-placeholder
```

For Firefox:

```
:-moz-placeholder
```

For WebKit browsers:

```
::-webkit-input-placeholder
```

Drawing primitives with CSS

Drawing primitives is the easiest and main case in graphic fundamentals. In CSS, it can be used in common cases such as adding details to buttons or any other DOM elements. Let's learn the basics of drawing primitives in CSS.

How to draw a rectangle/square

The easiest primitive to draw in CSS is a rectangle. Let's draw a simple rectangle using the following code:

HTML code:

```
<div class="rectangle"></div>
```

SASS code:

```
.rectangle
width: 100px
height: 200px
background: black
```

Compiled CSS:

```
.rectangle {
    width: 100px;
    height: 200px;
    background: black;
}
```

This will draw a rectangle in the browser as follows:

To draw a square, we need to create the following code:

HTML code:

```
<div class="square"></div>
```

SASS code:

```
.square
width: 100px
height: 100px
background: black
```

Compiled CSS:

```
.square {
    width: 100px;
    height: 100px;
    background: black;
}
```

Reusable mixins for square and rectangle:

```
=rectangle($w, $h, $c)
  width: $w
  height: $h
  background: $c

=square($w, $c)
  width: $w
  height: $w
  background: $c
```

How to draw a circle

Drawing a circle is pretty simple. The method is based on the border radius and a simple rectangle, which is shown in the following example:

HTML code:

```
<div class="circle"></div>
```

SASS code:

```
.circle
    width: 100px
    height: 100px
    border-radius: 50%
    background: black
```

Compiled CSS:

```
.circle {
    width: 100px;
    height: 100px;
    border-radius: 50%;
    background: black;
}
```

In the browser, you will see the following:

SASS mixin:

```
=circle($size, $color)
  width: $size
  height: $size
  border-radius: 50%
  background: $color
```

How to draw a ring

Drawing a ring is very similar to drawing a circle. The pattern is the same, but with a proper border. Let's start with the initial ring markup:

HTML code:

```
<div class="ring"></div>
```

SASS code:

```
.ring
  width: 100px
  height: 100px
  border-radius: 50%
  border: 2px solid black
  background: none
```

Compiled CSS:

```
.ring {
    width: 100px;
    height: 100px;
    border-radius: 50%;
    border: 2px solid black;
    background: none;
}
```

In the browser, you will see the following:

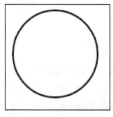

SASS mixin:

```
=ring($size, $color, $width)
  width: $size
height: $size
border-radius: 50%
  border: $width solid $color
background: none
```

How to draw a triangle with CSS

Drawing a triangle is based on a trick with borders:

HTML code:

```
<div class="triangle-up"></div><br>
<div class="triangle-down"></div><br>
<div class="triangle-left"></div><br>
<div class="triangle-right"></div>
```

The br elements are used only for displaying all elements in different lines.

SASS code:

```
.triangle-up
    width: 0
    height: 0
    border-left: 10px solid transparent
    border-right: 10px solid transparent
    border-bottom: 10px solid black

.triangle-down
    width: 0
    height: 0
    border-left: 10px solid transparent
    border-right: 10px solid transparent
    border-top: 10px solid black

.triangle-left
    width: 0
    height: 0
    border-top: 10px solid transparent
    border-bottom: 10px solid transparent
    border-left: 10px solid black
```

```
.triangle-right
    width: 0
    height: 0
    border-top: 10px solid transparent
    border-bottom: 10px solid transparent
    border-right: 10px solid black
```

Compiled CSS:

```
.triangle-up {
    width: 0;
    height: 0;
    border-left: 10px solid transparent;
    border-right: 10px solid transparent;
    border-bottom: 10px solid black;
}

.triangle-down {
    width: 0;
    height: 0;
    border-left: 10px solid transparent;
    border-right: 10px solid transparent;
    border-top: 10px solid black;
}

.triangle-left {
    width: 0;
    height: 0;
    border-top: 10px solid transparent;
    border-bottom: 10px solid transparent;
    border-left: 10px solid black;
}

.triangle-right {
    width: 0;
    height: 0;
    border-top: 10px solid transparent;
    border-bottom: 10px solid transparent;
    border-right: 10px solid black;
}
```

In the browser, you will see the following:

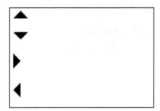

SASS mixins:

```
=triangleRight($width, $height, $color)
  width: 0
  height: 0
  border-style: solid
  border-width: $height/2 0 $height/2 $width
  border-color: transparent transparent transparent $color

=triangleLeft($width, $height, $color)
  width: 0
  height: 0
  border-style: solid
  border-width: $height/2 $width $height/2 0
  border-color: transparent $color transparent transparent

=triangleTop($width, $height, $color)
  width: 0
  height: 0
  border-style: solid
  border-width: 0 $width/2 $height $width/2
  border-color: transparent transparent $color transparent

=triangleBottom($width, $height, $color)
  width: 0
  height: 0
  border-style: solid
  border-width: $height $width/2 0 $width/2
  border-color: $color transparent transparent transparent
```

Pseudoelements

Using pseudoelements is really important to omit repeatable code elements that need specific HTML code. The main purpose of pseudoelements is to reduce DOM elements in the HTML code.

What is :before and :after?

:before and :after are pseudoelements that you can add to an HTML element. An element is added as an inline element into a selected element. To get the foundation of before and after pseudoelements, you can draw the HTML code as follows:

```
<a>Element</a>
```

And append the SASS code as follows:

```
a
  border: 1px solid #000

  &:before
    content: 'before'
    color: orange

  &:after
    content: 'after'
    color: orange
```

Compiled CSS:

```
a {
    border: 1px solid #000;
}

a:before {
    content: "before";
    color: orange;
}

a:after {
    content: "after";
    color: orange;
}
```

The output of the preceding code is as follows:

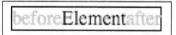

Where can we use :before and :after?

Let's assume a task where we need to apply to every element in a list some text at the end of the text. For example, we have a list like the following:

```
<ul>
    <li>Mike</li>
    <li>Ravi</li>
    <li>Adam</li>
    <li>Greg</li>
    <li>Anna</li>
</ul>
```

We need to add that each one is a frontend developer:

```
ul
   li
&:before
content: "My name is "
      color: #f00


&:after
content: ". I'm Front End Developer"
      color: #f00
```

Compiled CSS:

```
ul li:before {
    content: "My name is ";
    color: #f00;
}

ul li:after {
    content: ". I'm Front End Developer";
    color: #f00;
}
```

In the browser, you will see the following:

- My name is **Mike**. I'm Front End Developer
- My name is **Ravi**. I'm Front End Developer
- My name is **Adam**. I'm Front End Developer
- My name is **Greg**. I'm Front End Developer
- My name is **Anna**. I'm Front End Developer

Let's make our previous code reusable and let's create a button with an arrow at the right. The HTML code will look like the following:

```
<a href="#">Button</a>
```

Let's reuse our previously created mixin for triangle creation into the CSS code in the last line of the following SASS code:

```
=triangleRight($width, $height, $color)
  width: 0
  height: 0
  border-style: solid
  border-width: $height/2 0 $height/2 $width
  border-color: transparent transparent transparent $color


a
  display: inline-block
  border: 1px solid #000
    radius: 5px
  padding: 10px 40px 10px 10px
  position: relative
  text-decoration: none
  color: #000

  &:after
    display: block
    position: absolute
    right: 10px
    top: 50%
    margin-top: -5px
    content: ''
    +triangleRight(10px, 10px, #000)
```

Compiled CSS:

```
a {
    display: inline-block;
    border: 1px solid #000;
    border-radius: 5px;
    padding: 10px 40px 10px 10px;
    position: relative;
    text-decoration: none;
    color: #000;
```

```
    }

a:after {
    display: block;
    position: absolute;
    right: 10px;
    top: 50%;
    margin-top: -5px;
    content: "";
    width: 0;
    height: 0;
    border-style: solid;
    border-width: 5px 0 5px 10px;
    border-color: transparent transparent transparent #000;
}
```

It will give us the following result in the browser:

First letter and first line – simple text manipulation

On webpages, in some cases, you will need to add a style to the first line of the text and the first letter of the text. With CSS, you have to use the proper selector to do that. Let's use the following HTML code:

```
<p>Paragraph lorem ipsm Lorem ipsum dolor sit amet, consectetur
adipisicing elit. Totam nisi soluta doloribus ducimus repellat dolorum
quas atque, tempora quae, incidunt at eius eaque sit, culpa eum ut
corporis repudiandae.</p>
```

In SASS file:

```
p
  &:first-letter
    color: orange
    font:
      weight: bold
      size: 20px

  &:first-line
    color: pink
```

Compiled CSS:

```css
p:first-letter {
    color: orange;
    font-weight: bold;
    font-size: 20px;
}

p:first-line {
    color: pink;
}
```

The preceding code will change the color of the first line of the text to pink. The first letter will be changed to orange color, bold, and 20px size.

How to change selection color? Usage of ::selection

Companies have their own color palette. Sometimes you will need to customize the color of selection on the page. This is possible with the :selection pseudoelement:

SASS code:

```sass
::-moz-selection,
::selection
background: red
color: white
```

Compiled CSS:

```css
::-moz-selection,
::selection {
    background: red;
    color: white;
}
```

With the preceding code, every time you select something on the page, the selection will change its color to red and font color to white.

Summary

In this chapter, you learned the basics of pseudoclasses, pseudoelements, and the drawing of primitives in CSS code. As a front end developer, you will use these CSS elements very often. Pseudoclasses give you the basic interactivity (hover, active) and expand the possibilities of selectors (`:nth-child`, `:first-child`, `:last-child`). With pseudoelements, you can expand the possibilities of HTML with CSS code (`:before`, `:after`, `:first-letter`, `:first-line`) and you can set styles to selection.

In the next chapter, you will get basic knowledge about media queries, which are the foundation for responsive websites.

4
Responsive Websites – Prepare Your Code for Specific Devices

In this chapter, you will gain knowledge about **responsive web design** (RWD) and how to prepare projects. It will cover problems of modern websites and optimization techniques. This chapter will be the base of knowledge about media queries—how to prepare them and how to adjust specific devices.

In this chapter, we will cover the following topics:

- RWD methodologies
- Using media queries

The foundation of responsive websites

Almost all modern websites can be displayed on desktop and mobile devices (phones, tablets). Proper adjusting of CSS and HTML code is the main assumption for creating a responsive website. The basic responsive website building process was based on adjustments of code, which once done, the site properly displayed on all devices. Now the *responsiveness* of responsive websites is a little bit enhanced. It's not only the creation of CSS/HTML/JS code and thinking about the design aspects but also the thinking about performance on mobile devices. Mobile devices with a web browser are now the main equipment on which people browse websites. Let's look at the main approaches for creating responsive websites.

Desktop first methodology

This methodology was used back in the day as the main approach in CSS frameworks. The main purpose of HTML and CSS code was to see a web page in a desktop browser. Then provide the mobile version which was based on the desktop code. The final process was about adjusting the code for mobiles. It seemed like cutting the functionality of the website and adjusting the desktop view for a smaller mobile gadget.

Mobile first methodology

This methodology is used in all modern CSS frameworks (Twitter bootstrap, Foundation framework). Firstly, code is prepared for mobile devices and then it's *scaled* for larger devices, from tablets to desktop screens. This approach is more common right now and is better because code for mobile devices doesn't have to be a combination of CSS tricks, HTML duplications, and JS mechanisms like it was in the desktop first methodology.

Which methodology is proper for you? It all depends on the project type. Not in all cases you are making a project from beginning to end. Sometimes, you have some legacy code, which you need to adjust to mobile. In this case, you are always forced to use the desktop first methodology. In cases in which you can write code from scratch, it is recommended to use the mobile first methodology.

Adjusting the viewport in HTML

An important element of responsive websites is the proper HTML viewport meta tag. A viewport description should be added in the head section of an HTML document. It describes how webpage should behave on mobile devices. There is a bunch of mostly used viewports, which we will analyze later. The mostly used is the viewport that looks like the following:

```
<head>
    <!-- ... -->
    <meta name="viewport" content="width=device-width, initial-
scale=1.0">
    <!-- ... -->
</head>
```

It means that whenever you open your project on a mobile device, it will have the width of the device and the project will have an initial scale equal to 1. A little bit more enhanced viewport looks like the following:

```
<head>
    <!-- ... -->
```

```
    <meta name="viewport"content="width=device-width, initial-
scale=2.0">
    <!-- ... -->
</head>
```

The main difference between the first and second viewports is the max scale. This means that after a zoom action, which is invoked after a double tap on a mobile device or a pinch gesture, it will be scaled, but the maximum range of this scale is set to 2. A safer option for a viewport is as follows:

```
<head>
    <!-- ... -->
    <meta name="viewport"content="width=device-width, initial-
scale=1.0, maximum-scale=1">
    <!-- ... -->
</head>
```

Why safer? For example, in cases in which we have some fixed windows over the content, they won't be scaled too and won't deliver a bad experience for the user:

```
<head>
    <!-- ... -->
    <meta name="viewport"content="width=600, initial-scale=1.0">
    <!-- ... -->
</head>
```

This `viewport` setting will scale the website such that it will behave like a webpage opened on a desktop, with a set width of browser equal to `600`. The initial scale is set like in preceding example and is equal to `1`.

Choosing the right viewport

So the question is: which `viewport` is recommended? This is a good question. The best experience can be preserved with the following:

```
<head>
    <!-- ... -->
    <meta name="viewport"content="width=device-width, initial-
scale=1.0, maximum-scale=2.0">
    <!-- ... -->
</head>
```

Why? Because we are scaling the website to the device `width` and we are not stopping the zooming of the page. But the safest choice is as follows:

```
<head>
    <!-- ... -->
```

```
    <meta name="viewport"content="width=device-width, initial-
scale=1.0, maximum-scale=1">
    <!-- ... -->
</head>
```

This will prevent zooming, which can be annoying to adjust, especially in old projects in which we have old school types of modal windows.

Above the fold

This methodology is strictly connected with optimization of your code. It's related to the mobile and desktop versions of webpages also. Modern webpages load a lot of stuff: CSS files, JS files, images, and media files such as videos and sounds. With such a long queue, you can see that when the processing time of page loading is, for example, 10 seconds long, you cannot see the content till all files are loaded. In the case of informational pages, you should see the header and main content first, but it is almost impossible in such a long queue.

The aforementioned fold methodology separates specific style attachments, which describe the most important elements on the page, such as title, subtitle, and text content. It needs to separate these `style` attachments and include them inline in the `head` section, for example:

```
<head>
    <!-- ... -->
    <style>
        /* here we have a section for inline most important styles */
    </style>
    <!-- ... -->
    <link rel="stylesheet"type="text/css"href="link_to_rest_of_styles.
css">
    <!-- ... -->
</head>
```

It means that this inline section will be first parsed by the browser and, in the long loading process, it will first prepare the most important elements for the reader and then will load the rest of needed by page resources.

Media queries – where can you use it

Media queries are filters set in CSS code, which help to describe the website for a bunch of displays (screen, print). In media queries, the mostly used filters are min/max width, min/max height, min/max pixel ratio, and min/max aspect ratio.

How to build media queries

It's pretty simple to first create a media query and then create more complicated filters. The basic media query looks like the following:

```
@media screen and (min-width: 640px)
  .element
    background: #000
```

Compiled CSS:

```
@media screen and (min-width: 640px) {
    .element {
        background: #000;
    }
}
```

With this media query, you are filtering all CSS declarations for a screen whose minimal width is 640px. Let's try to make it more complex and let's try to create some more media queries for specific devices.

How media queries work?

Media queries are filters, as mentioned previously. But let's try to see it in code and browser. This simple chapter will show you how to adjust the code for specific screen resolutions and will be the foundation for creating more advanced media queries:

```
<div class="mobile_only">Mobile only</div>
<div class="tablet_only">Tablet only</div>
<div class="desktop_only">Desktop only</div>
<div class="mobile_and_tablet">Mobile and tablet</div>
<div class="tablet_and_desktop">Tablet and desktop</div>
<div class="all">All views</div>
```

The code will now look like the following (without any styling):

Mobile only
Tablet only
Desktop only
Mobile and tablet
Tablet and desktop
All views

Now we need to make some approaches:

- Mobile view is all resolutions to 400px in width
- Tablet view is all resolutions to 700px in width
- Desktop view is all resolutions since 701px in width

Now, based on the preceding approaches, let's create style and media queries:

Compiled CSS:

```css
.mobile_only,
.tablet_only,
.desktop_only,
.mobile_and_tablet,
.tablet_and_desktop {
    display: none;
}

/* Mobile only */
@media screen and (max-width: 400px) {
body {
        background: red;
    }

    .mobile_only {
        display: block;
    }
}

/* Mobile and tablet */
@media screen and (max-width: 700px) {
    .mobile_and_tablet {
        display: block;
    }
}
```

```
/* Tablet only */
@media screen and (min-width: 401px) and (max-width: 700px) {
body {
        background: blue;
    }

    .tablet_only {
        display: block;
    }
}

/* Tablet and desktop */
@media screen and (min-width: 401px) {
    .tablet_and_desktop {
        display: block;
    }
}

/* Desktop only */
@media screen and (min-width: 701px) {
body {
        background: green;
    }

    .desktop_only {
        display: block;
    }
}
```

Now let's check it in a browser with 350px width:

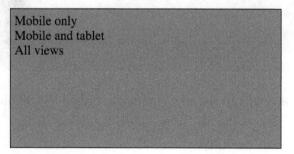

In the preceding view, we can see all elements described in CSS files with the following comments:

- /* Mobile only */
- /* Mobile and tablet */

The output of a browser with 550px width will be as follows:

In the preceding view, we can see all elements described in CSS files with the following comments:

- `/* Tablet only */`
- `/* Mobile and tablet */`
- `/* Tablet and desktop */`

The output in a browser with 850px width is as follows:

Desktop only
Tablet and desktop
All views

In the preceding view, we can see all elements described in CSS files with the following comments:

- `/* Tablet and desktop */`
- `/* Desktop only*/`

The previous code reveals how the media query filters are working exactly. How can you create a code that will be visible in specific views and how can you create approaches for real projects? In the next projects, we will study what we can filter because media queries are not only related to the width of the device. Let's begin!

Media queries for specific views/devices

Media queries can be used in many different cases. As mentioned previously, we can use media queries for specific min and max width:

```
@media screen and (min-width: 640px)
@media screen and (max-width: 640px)
```

In the preceding media queries, the first example is for all resolutions with min-width 640 pixels and the second one is for all resolutions with max-width 640 pixels. Frontend developers deals with pixel ratios on basic desktops and screens with a bigger density, such as retina. How to filter them with CSS? Let's check this media query:

```
@media (-webkit-min-device-pixel-ratio: 2)
```

As we know, retina devices have a pixel ratio equal to 2. We can also build more complicated filters with ranges:

```
@media screen and (min-width: 640px) and (max-width: 1024px)
```

In this case, we are filtering all resolutions whose width matches the filter min-width 640 pixels to 1024 pixels. But how can we write a media query filter that will match some specific devices? Let's assume that we want to write code for new-generation iPad with retina display:

```
@media only screen
and (min-device-width: 768px)
and (max-device-width: 1024px)
and (-webkit-min-device-pixel-ratio: 2)
```

As we know, mobile devices have two orientations: landscape and portrait. So how can we match this case in media queries? For portrait view, use the following:

```
@media only screen
and (min-device-width: 768px)
and (max-device-width: 1024px)
and (orientation: portrait)
and (-webkit-min-device-pixel-ratio: 2)
```

And for landscape view, use the following:

```
@media only screen
and (min-device-width: 768px)
and (max-device-width: 1024px)
and (orientation: landscape)
and (-webkit-min-device-pixel-ratio: 1)
```

With media queries, you can filter print views also. To do so, you need to append the code like the following:

```
@media print
```

How to choose proper media queries for mobile devices

For creating a good filter in media queries and setting good ranges in them, you have to first choose the devices and resolutions. Then you have to create proper media queries based on the most trendy resolutions. Back in the day, there was a smaller spectrum of devices and standard resolutions. So the main settings were as follows:

```
@media (max-width: 768px)
  // Cover small devices
  .element
    font-size: 12px

@media (min-width: 768px) and (max-width: 1024px)
  // Cover medium devices
  .element
    font-size: 14px

@media (min-width: 1024px)
  // Cover large devices
  .element
    font-size: 16px
```

Compiled CSS:

```
@media (max-width: 768px) {
    .element {
        font-size: 12px;
    }
}

@media (min-width: 768px) and (max-width: 1024px) {
    .element {
        font-size: 14px;
    }
}

@media (min-width: 1024px) {
    .element {
```

```
    font-size: 16px;
  }
}
```

Of course, in every project, you could add some *specific* media queries for exceptions so that after the quality analysis process, there could appear more of the filters in CSS file.

Nowadays, the approach is to cover as many devices as possible in one step of media query:

```
@media only screen
  .element
    font-size: 16px
@media only screen and (max-width: 640px)
  // Cover small devices
  .element
    font-size: 12px

@media only screen and (min-width: 641px)
  // Cover devices which resolution is at minimum medium
  .element
    font-size: 14px

@media only screen and (min-width: 641px) and (max-width: 1024px)
  // Cover medium devices
  .element
    font-size: 15px

@media only screen and (min-width: 1025px)
  // Cover  devices which resolution is at minimum large
  .element
    font-size: 16px
```

Compiled CSS:

```
@media only screen {
    .element {
        font-size: 16px;
    }
}

@media only screen and (max-width: 640px) {
    .element {
        font-size: 12px;
    }
```

```
    }

    @media only screen and (min-width: 641px) {
        .element {
            font-size: 14px;
        }
    }

    @media only screen and (min-width: 641px) and (max-width: 1024px) {
        .element {
            font-size: 15px;
        }
    }

    @media only screen and (min-width: 1025px) {
        .element {
            font-size: 16px;
        }
    }
```

For better coverage and better code writing, let's add to this media queries list one `max-width` step:

```
    @media only screen and (max-width: 1024px)
        .element
            font-size: 15px
```

Compiled CSS:

```
    @media only screen and (min-width: 1025px) {
        .element {
            font-size: 16px;
        }
    }
```

This media query will cover small and medium devices at once. Currently, the most known resolution of desktop websites is `1280px`. Let's add this range to the media queries:

```
    @media only screen and (min-width: 1025px) and (max-width: 1280px) {}
    @media only screen and (min-width: 1281px) {}
```

SASS mixins for media queries

Let's create media queries for mixins, which will help us to keep the code clear. As we know, we have to add the display type and the breakpoint as parameters:

```
@mixin mq($display, $breakpoint)
@media #{$display} and (#{$breakpoint})
@content
```

Now let's gather our standard breakpoints:

```
@mixin mq($display, $breakpoint)
  @media #{$display} and #{$breakpoint}
    @content


$mq_small_only: "(max-width: 640px)"
$mq_medium_only: "(min-width: 641px) and (max-width: 1024px)"
$mq_small_and_medium: "(max-width: 1024px)"

+mq("screen", $mq_small_only)
  .slider
    width: 100%
    height: 300px

+mq("screen", $mq_medium_only)
  .slider
    width: 100%
    height: 400px

+mq("screen", $mq_small_and_medium)
  .slider
    max-width: 1200px
    width: 100%
```

Compiled CSS:

```
@media screen and (max-width: 640px) {
    .slider {
        width: 100%;
        height: 300px;
    }
}

@media screen and (min-width: 641px) and (max-width: 1024px) {
    .slider {
        width: 100%;
        height: 400px;
    }
```

```
    }

@media screen and (max-width: 1024px) {
    .slider {
        max-width: 1200px;
        width: 100%;
    }
}
```

The preceding code is a choice of three steps, but you can add another as an exercise to cover all steps from the previous section.

Usage sample – main navigation

Let's imagine that we want to resolve the classic problem related to navigation. It is in most cases inline in desktop view, but it is changed in mobile views into list element under element. Let's start with HTML:

```html
<nav class="main-navigation">
    <ul>
        <li>
            <a href="#">First element</a>
        </li>
        <li>
            <a href="#">Second element</a>
        </li>
        <li>
            <a href="#"> Third element</a>
        </li>
    </ul>
</nav>
```

In SASS code, we will use previously created mixins for media queries and clear fix. The following is the full SASS file:

```
@mixin mq($display, $breakpoint)
@media #{$display} and #{$breakpoint}
@content

$mq_small_only: "(max-width: 640px)"
$mq_medium_only: "(min-width: 641px) and (max-width: 1024px)"
$mq_small_and_medium: "(max-width: 1024px)"

=clear fix
  &:after
```

```
      content: " "
      visibility: hidden
      display: block
      height: 0
      clear: both

body
  padding: 0
  margin: 0

.main-navigation
  ul
    +clearfix /* This will prevent problems of cleared float */
    list-style: none
    padding: 0
    background: greenyellow
    border:
      bottom: 1px solid darkgreen


  li
    float: left
    display: block

  a
    padding: 10px
    width: 100%
    display: block
    background: greenyellow
    text-decoration: none
    color: darkgreen

    &:hover
      background: darkgreen
      color: greenyellow


+mq("screen", $mq_small_and_medium)
  .main-navigation
    ul
      list-style: none
      border: none

    li
```

```
        float: none
        width: 100%

   a
     border:
       bottom: 1px solid darkgreen
```

Compiled CSS:

```css
body {
    padding: 0;
    margin: 0;
}

.main-navigation ul {
    list-style: none;
    padding: 0;
    background: greenyellow;
    border-bottom: 1px solid darkgreen;
}

.main-navigation ul:after {
    content: "";
    visibility: hidden;
    display: block;
    height: 0;
    clear: both;
}

.main-navigation li {
    float: left;
    display: block;
}

.main-navigation a {
    padding: 10px;
    width: 100%;
    display: block;
    background: greenyellow;
    text-decoration: none;
    color: darkgreen;
}

.main-navigation a:hover {
    background: darkgreen;
```

```
        color: greenyellow;
    }

@media screen and (max-width: 1024px) {
    .main-navigation ul {
        list-style: none;
        border: none;
    }

    .main-navigation li {
        float: none;
        width: 100%;
    }

    .main-navigation a {
        border-bottom: 1px solid darkgreen;
    }
}
```

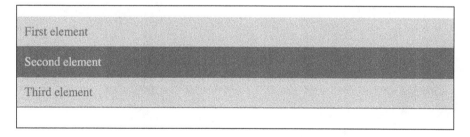

The preceding screenshot is made in desktop view related to global CSS. The next screenshot is related to @media screen and (max-width: 1024px). As you can see, we changed the method of display of the navigation and additionally gave more flexibility for touch devices. The bigger items in navigation are easier to click (in this example, the buttons are longer):

Summary

In this chapter, you learned the main approaches for creating responsive websites and what mobile and desktop first mean. Then we expanded the knowledge with the basics of performance of responsive websites. Finally, you gained basic knowledge about media queries and how to create them to cover all specific display types. In the next chapter, you will gain knowledge about images in CSS code.

In the next chapter, you will also gain knowledge about CSS backgrounds and new features that you can use. We will be repeating images, cutting images, and positioning them into the container. Let's check what we can do with backgrounds.

5

Using Background Images in CSS

Background images are on almost all pages. This chapter will describe how to craft an optimal website with images displayed correctly on the wide spectrum of modern devices including mobile phones and tablets.

In this chapter, we will cover the following topics:

- Usage of background images
- How to set proper position for background images
- How to set the size of a background position
- Images on retina and mobile devices

CSS backgrounds

CSS backgrounds are very useful in modern web browsers. When should you use a background and when should you use the `img` tag? It's a simple question—every image that is an element of content should be inserted into the `img` tag and every image that is an element of a layout should be moved to the CSS background.

In this chapter, we will try to always use the same image to illustrate how each property and value is working. This image will be a bordered circle that will definitely show the correct aspect ratio (if it is bad, it will look more like ellipsis), and with the border, you can check how the repeating of images will work. The width and height of the image are equal to 90 pixels.

Repeating of background

There are many options available when working with a background. The first is image repeat. The default value is to repeat an image in both the *x* and *y* axes. So when you set, for example:

```
Background-image: url(/* here url to your img*/)
```

Our SASS example:

```
.container
  width: 1000px
  height: 500px
  border: 3px solid red
  background-image: url(image.jpg)
```

Compiled CSS:

```
.container {
    width: 1000px;
    height: 500px;
    border: 3px solid red;
    background-image: url(image.jpg);
}
```

For all containers, the border is red so as to allow a better view of the scope of the container.

HTML:

```
<body>
<div class="container">

</div>
</body>
```

This code will bring us the following view:

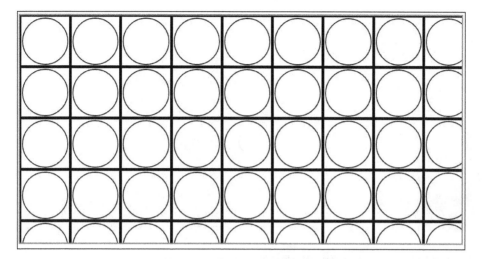

For all containers, the border is red so as to allow a better view of the scope of the container. It means that the image is repeated in the background in both x and y axes. Let's add the following code and check how it will compile and what impact on our view we will see:

```
.container
  width: 1000px
  height: 500px
  border: 3px solid red
  background:
    image: url(image.jpg)
    repeat: repeat
```

Compiled CSS:

```
.container {
    width: 1000px;
    height: 500px;
    border: 3px solid red;
    background-image: url(image.jpg);
    background-repeat: repeat;
}
```

Another option that we can use and the behavior of `background-repeat`:

- • - `repeat-x`: This will repeat background *x* axis

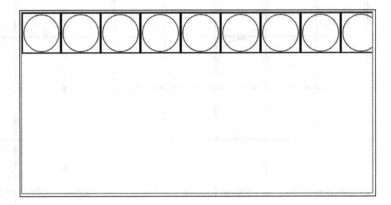

- • - `repeat-y`: This will repeat background *y* axis

- • - `no-repeat`: This will not repeat the background

Background size

With new CSS features, you can set the background size. Size can be set as follows:

```
background-size: 30px 50px
```

Let's get the previous HTML code and append the new SASS code:

```
.container
  width: 1000px
  height: 500px
  border: 3px solid red
  background:
    image: url(image.jpg)
    repeat: repeat
    size: 30px 50px
```

Compiled CSS:

```
.container {
    width: 1000px;
    height: 500px;
    border: 3px solid red;
    background-image: url(image.jpg);
    background-repeat: repeat;
    background-size: 30px 50px;
}
```

The output of this code will be as follows:

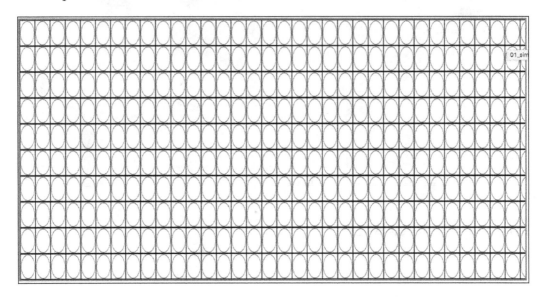

If we want to set the full width of the container for an image and automatically count its height to maintain the aspect ratio of image, perform the following:

```
background-size: 100% auto
```

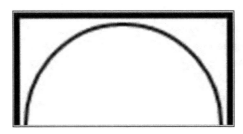

We can, of course, change the `fill` option from the *x* axis to the *y* axis. Let's change the `100%` value to `height` and `auto` for `width`:

```
.container
    width: 1000px
    height: 500px
    border: 3px solid red
```

```
background:
    image: url(image.jpg)
    repeat: repeat
    size: 100% auto
```

Compiled to:

```
.container {
    width: 1000px;
    height: 500px;
    border: 3px solid red;
    background-image: url(image.jpg);
    background-repeat: repeat;
    background-size: 100% auto;
}
```

The output will be as follows:

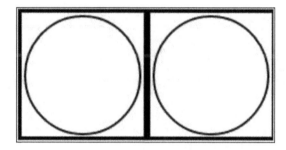

The contain value will change its width and height to contain the container. With this option, the aspect ratio will be maintained:

```
background-size: contain
```

The cover value will change its width and height to cover the container. With this option, the aspect ratio will be maintained:

```
background-size: cover
```

Background position

In most designs, you will need to set the position of the background in a box. The background position can be set with CSS as follows:

```
background-position: top left
```

```
background-position: right
```

If you want to center the position of the background in both axes perform the following:

```
background-position: center center
```

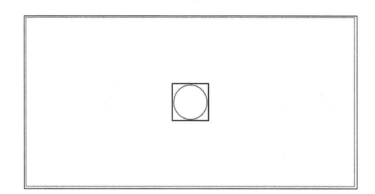

If you want to align the background to bottom right perform the following:

```
background-position: bottom right
```

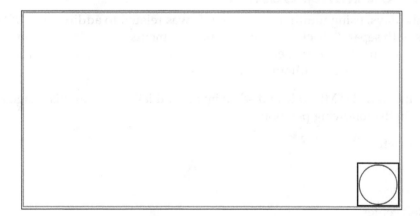

To set the background offset in pixels perform the following:

```
background-position: 600px 200px
```

Multiple backgrounds

Back in the days, using multiple backgrounds was related to adding new DOM elements with separate backgrounds. All these elements would be positioned absolutely in a relative container. Nowadays, we can use multiple backgrounds in one container using CSS without any additional HTML code.

Let's use the same HTML code and same image and let's position this image in a container in the following positions:

- top left
- top center
- top right
- left center
- center center
- right center
- bottom left
- bottom center
- bottom right

CSS code:

```
.container {
width: 1000px;
height: 500px;
border: 3px solid red;
background-image:
        url(image.jpg), /* URL of image #1 */
        url(image.jpg), /* URL of image #2 */
        url(image.jpg), /* URL of image #3 */
        url(image.jpg), /* URL of image #4 */
        url(image.jpg), /* URL of image #5 */
        url(image.jpg), /* URL of image #6 */
        url(image.jpg), /* URL of image #7 */
        url(image.jpg), /* URL of image #8 */
        url(image.jpg); /* URL of image #9 */
background-repeat: no-repeat;
background-position:
        left top, /* position of image #1 */
        center top, /* position of image #2 */
        right top, /* position of image # 3*/
        left center, /* position of image #4 */
        center center, /* position of image #5 */
        right center, /* position of image #6 */
        bottom left, /* position of image #7 */
        bottom center, /* position of image #8 */
        bottom right; /* position of image #1 */
background-size:
        50px auto, /* size of image #1 */
        auto auto, /* size of image #2 */
        auto auto, /* size of image #3 */
        auto auto, /* size of image #4 */
        200px auto, /* size of image #5 */
        auto auto, /* size of image #6 */
        auto auto, /* size of image #7 */
        auto auto, /* size of image #8 */
        50px auto; /* size of image #9 */
}
```

Now, let's describe it in SASS:

```
.container
  width: 1000px
  height: 500px
  border: 3px solid red
  background:
    image: url(image.jpg), url(image.jpg), url(image.jpg), url(image.
jpg), url(image.jpg),url(image.jpg), url(image.jpg), url(image.jpg),
url(image.jpg)
    repeat: no-repeat
    position: left top, center top, right top, left center, center
center, right center, bottom left, bottom center, bottom right
    size: 50px auto, auto auto, auto auto, auto auto, 200px auto, auto
auto, auto auto, auto auto, 50px auto
```

The final view will be as shown in the following:

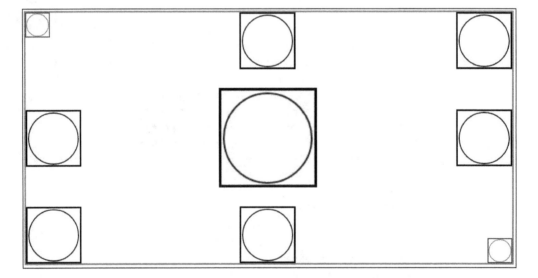

How to create and use sprites

What is a sprite? A sprite is an image with images in short. But how can you use it in your code and why should you use it in your CSS? Because it can make your website faster and it is rather simple to create. Let's check the following image:

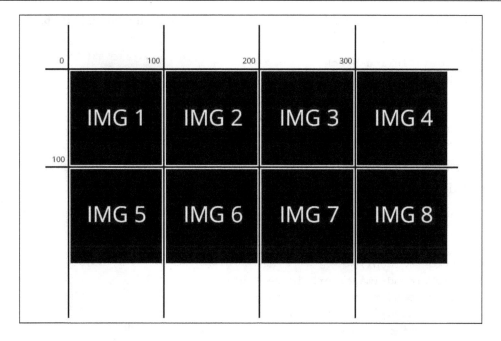

This is a basic sprite with set offsets in the x and y axes. So how can we extract **IMG 3** from this big image?

```
.image3
  display: inline-block
  width: 100px
  height: 100px
  background:
    image: url(image.jpg)
    repeat: no-repeat
    position: -200px 0
```

Compiled CSS:

```
.image3 {
    display: inline-block;
    width: 100px;
    height: 100px;
    background-image: url(image.jpg);
    background-repeat: no-repeat;
    background-position: -200px 0;
}
```

To understand the sprite grid better, let's get the object with the name **IMG 6**:

```
.image6
  display: inline-block
  width: 100px
  height: 100px
  background:
    image: url(image.jpg)
    repeat: no-repeat
    position: -200px -100px
```

Compiled:

```
.image6 {
    display: inline-block;
    width: 100px;
    height: 100px;
    background-image: url(image.jpg);
    background-repeat: no-repeat;
    background-position: -200px -100px;
}
```

Okay. But creating sprites is pretty boring and time-consuming. How can this process be automatized? It's pretty easy with Compass. All we need to do is to gather all the images in a folder with the name `newsprite`. The best format for sprites is PNG to keep the proper transparency. Let's assume that we have the following three PNG files in this folder:

- `circle-blue.png`
- `circle-red.png`
- `circle-white.png`

The images will be as follows:

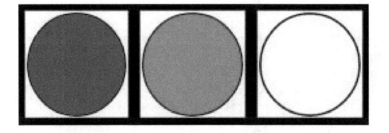

Now we will need to add a little change into our automatizer:

```
var gulp = require('gulp'),
    compass = require('gulp-compass');

gulp.task('compass', function () {
    return gulp.src('src/styles/main.sass')
        .pipe(compass({
            sass: 'src/styles',
            image: 'src/images',
            css: 'dist/css',
            generated_images_path: 'dist/images',
            sourcemap: true,
            style: 'compressed'
        }))
        .on('error', function(err) {
            console.log(err);
        });
});


gulp.task('default', function () {
    gulp.watch('src/styles/**/*.sass', ['compass']);
    gulp.watch('src/images/**/*', ['compass']);
});
```

We changed the following line, which defines the destination for images:

```
generated_images_path: 'dist/images'
```

Now we need to add a code to the run sprite creator in `compass`:

```
@import "compass"
@import "newsprite/*.png"
@include all-newsprite-sprites(true)
```

In the first line of the preceding code, we are importing the `compass` library. In the second line, we are mapping our images as `sprites`. In the third line, we are importing a folder with `sprites`. The value in brackets gives dimensions in classes in compiled CSS code. Now let's analyze the compiled CSS:

```
.newsprite-sprite,
.newsprite-circle-blue,
.newsprite-circle-red,
.newsprite-circle-white {
```

```
    background-image: url('../images/newsprite-s70c66611b2.png');
    background-repeat: no-repeat
}

.newsprite-circle-blue {
    background-position: 0 0;
    height: 90px;
    width: 90px
}

.newsprite-circle-red {
    background-position: 0 -90px;
    height: 90px;
    width: 90px
}

.newsprite-circle-white {
    background-position: 0 -180px;
    height: 90px;
    width: 90px
}
```

As you can see, the generated code is related to the files structure and names, for example:

```
.newsprite-circle-red
```

Where:

- `newsprite`: This is a folder/sprite name
- `circle-white`: This is file name

Compass is prefixing the generated sprite image, for example:

```
background-image: url('../images/newsprite-s70c66611b2.png');
```

And the generated file:

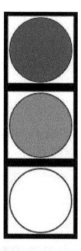

Now let's change the code a little bit and let's use sprite-map. Firstly, we will need to create HTML code to finally see the effect in browser:

```
<div class="element-circle-white"></div>
<div class="element-circle-red"></div>
<div class="element-circle-blue"></div>
```

Then in SASS file:

```
@import "compass/utilities/sprites"

$circles: sprite-map("newsprite/*.png", $spacing: 2px, $layout:
diagonal)

.element-circle-blue
  background-image: sprite-url($circles)
  background-position: sprite-position($circles, circle-blue)
  @include sprite-dimensions($circles, circle-blue)

.element-circle-red
  background-image: sprite-url($circles)
  background-position: sprite-position($circles, circle-red)
  @include sprite-dimensions($circles, circle-red)

.element-circle-white
  background-image: sprite-url($circles)
  background-position: sprite-position($circles, circle-white)
  @include sprite-dimensions($circles, circle-white)
```

```
.element-circle-blue,
.element-circle-red,
.element-circle-white
  float: left
```

Generated CSS:

```css
.element-circle-blue {
    background-image: url('../images/newsprite-s31a73c8e82.png');
    background-position: 0 -180px;
    height: 90px;
    width: 90px
}

.element-circle-red {
    background-image: url('../images/newsprite-s31a73c8e82.png');
    background-position: -90px -90px;
    height: 90px;
    width: 90px
}

.element-circle-white {
    background-image: url('../images/newsprite-s31a73c8e82.png');
    background-position: -180px 0;
    height: 90px;
    width: 90px
}

.element-circle-blue, .element-circle-red, .element-circle-white {
    float: left
}
```

In the preceding code, we are not adding all classes with their dimensions like we did previously. This is important when you do not want to add a lot of unused code. Now we are only using the part of sprite that is needed. Let's analyze it a little deeper:

```
$circles: sprite-map("newsprite/*.png", $spacing: 2px, $layout:
diagonal)
```

This line of code defines our image (which was @import "newsprite/*.png"). The second parameter defines the spacing between images in sprite ($spacing: 2px); in this case it is 2px. And the last parameter is defining the layout style. In this case, the images in sprite will look like the following:

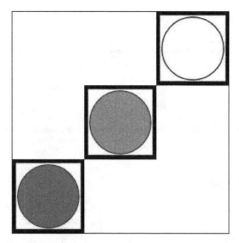

With this parameter, we can use the following values:

- **Vertical**: Elements of sprite will be placed in one vertical line
- **Horizontal**: Elements of sprite will be placed in a horizontal line
- **Diagonal**: Elements of sprite will be placed in a diagonal line
- **Smart**: Elements will be adjusted to get at as small an area as it is possible

Let's analyze the next part of the code:

```
background-image: sprite-url($circles)
background-position: sprite-position($circles, circle-red)
@include sprite-dimensions($circles, circle-red)
```

In the first line of the preceding code, we are getting the `$circle` variable, which is defined as follows:

```
$circles: sprite-map("newsprite/*.png", $spacing: 2px, $layout:
diagonal)
```

This line adds the background image. The second line is getting the position of the image with name `circle-red` defined in the `$circle` variable (sprite). The last line includes the width and height of `circle-red` in this class.

In the browser, we can see the following view:

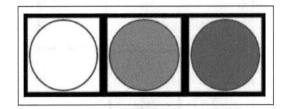

Usage of base64

This is a technique strictly connected with page load optimization and minification of requests sent to the server. Conceptually, optimization was related with making count requests as small as possible. So let's assume that we have 10 image backgrounds, which we need to load on a page. The first request is for CSS and the next 10 requests to the server are for images. But how can we make it work in one request? We can use base64 coding.

Let's observe at how it looks in theory:

```
data:[<mime type>][;charset=<charset>][;base64],<encoded data>
```

This is the main method in which we encode the image. Finally, it looks like the following:

```
background-image: url(data:image/gif;base64,<encoded data>)
```

Hey! But how can I change my image to encoded data? This is an excellent question at a great time. Open your terminal and try to do it with the following command:

```
openssl base64 -in <imgfile> -out <outputfile>
```

After this operation, all you need to do is to copy the output file content to <encode data> from the previous command.

Retina problems

Retina is the high-resolution display. The only problem with this display is how to double the device width and height and then squeeze it into the keeping container. This sounds easy. The easiest way is to move as many elements as can be moved to fonts and HTML elements/pseudoelements. But how can we deal with background images in CSS?

Let's start with the basics. For a normal screen, we need the image with standard dimensions. The image width and height are equal to 90 pixels.

HTML:

```
<div class="element"></div>
```

SASS:

```
.element
  background:
    image: url(img/circle-blue.png)
    repeat: no-repeat
  width: 90px
  height: 90px
```

Complied CSS:

```
.element {
    background-image: url(img/circle-blue.png);
    background-repeat: no-repeat;
    width: 90px;
    height: 90px;
}
```

In case we want to display this image properly on the retina display, we need to change a code. This change is related with the density of the retina display. The pixel ratio in the retina display is equal to 2. All we need to change is the width and height of the element and adjust the background image in this box:

```
.element
  background:
    image: url(img/circle-blue.png)
    repeat: no-repeat
    size: 50% 50%
  width: 45px
  height: 45px
```

Compiled CSS:

```
.element {
    background-image: url(img/circle-blue.png);
    background-repeat: no-repeat;
    background-size: 50% 50%;
    width: 45px;
    height: 45px;
}
```

Now `.element` is ready to display on the retina display with the correct quality. But it will be two times smaller than needed. All we need to do in this case is to start with a bigger resolution of the image—it should be two times bigger. For example, the design is prepared for the browser, and in the browser, the main wrapper width should be 1000px; so you should ask the designer to design the width of this wrapper equal to 200px. In bigger designs, you are cutting slices, which will be needed on the retina display. Then you should cut images for standard density. You can leave only the retina images but it can affect performance because bigger images will always be downloaded in the browser. To omit this problem, it is good to add a proper media query. In the described example, we are globally adding a normal version of the file (`img/circle-blue.png`) in the case of the retina display, which is recognized by the media query so that a two times bigger image will be loaded (`img/circle-blue@2x.png`).

```
.element
  background:
    image: url(img/circle-blue.png)
    repeat: no-repeat
  width: 45px
  height: 45px


@media (-webkit-min-device-pixel-ratio: 2), (min-resolution: 192dpi)
  .element
    background:
      image: url(img/circle-blue@2x.png)
      repeat: no-repeat
      size: 50% 50%
    width: 45px
    height: 45px
```

Compiled CSS:

```
.element {
    background-image: url(img/circle-blue.png);
    background-repeat: no-repeat;
    width: 45px;
    height: 45px;
}

@media (-webkit-min-device-pixel-ratio: 2), (min-resolution: 192dpi) {
    .element {
        background-image: url(img/circle-blue@2x.png);
        background-repeat: no-repeat;
        background-size: 50% 50%;
```

```
        width: 45px;
        height: 45px;
    }
}
```

Take the following part of the code:

```
background-size: 50% 50%
```

This part of code can be swapped with the following:

```
background-size: contain
```

The image in this case will adjust to the width and height of the box into which the background is added.

Summary

In this chapter, you gained a basic knowledge about background images. You also learned how to position background images, set their sizes, and how to resolve the main performance problems with `sprites` and `base64` encoding.

In the next chapter, you will gain basic knowledge about the styling of forms. You will also gain in-depth knowledge about treating inputs with CSS code.

6
Styling Forms

Styling forms is one of the most challenging tasks, especially when the form needs to be created as desktop and mobile. Why?

In this chapter, we will cover the following topics:

- How to create a good structure for easy styling
- Using form selectors
- How to style forms
- What is possible and what not with CSS in forms

Forms – the most known issues

Do you know any frontend developer who hasn't built any form in HTML/CSS? Do you know any of them who like to do this work? Yeah… It's not simple to adjust it, but you need to learn to understand what you can do with HTML/CSS and where you need to use JavaScript code to make it easier or even possible.

The most known restrictions are as follows:

- Usage of pseudoelements `:before` and `:after` is not allowed because the input has no content (`:before` and `:after` appear before or after the content)
- Usage of global input styles is not good because of lots of types of inputs (text, password, submit)
- Styling of displayed elements in the selected box is not possible at all (sometimes it is easier to use some JavaScript plugin to enable additional structure, which is easier for styling)

Forms – enable superpowers

As mentioned previously, in the input, there is no way to use `:before` and `:after` pseudoelements. But a quick trick to do that, which will be better described in the following sections, is to wrap it in some other elements. It always helps to keep some label and input groups and additionally allows to append the `:before` and `:after` pseudoelements.

For example, take the following bare HTML form code:

```
<form>
    <input type="text" placeholder="Login"/>
    <input type="password" placeholder="Password"/>
</form>
```

Now you just need to add wrapping elements:

```
<form>
    <div class="inputKeeper">
        <input type="text" placeholder="Login"/>
    </div>
    <div class="inputKeeper">
        <input type="password" placeholder="Password"/>
    </div>
</form>
```

Where is the difference? It is easy to see it. The first form output is as follows:

The second form is as follows:

How to style simple input

Styling input is based on the selectors `<input>` `<select>` `<textarea>`. But there is a problem with `<input>` types. It will gather all types:

```
<input type="text">
<input type="submit">
<input type="password">
<input type="checkbox">
```

For password input:

```
input[type="password"]
For submit input:
input[type="submit"]
```

Let's gather these inputs into one mostly appeared on websites' login form.

HTML code:

```
<form>
    <input type="text" placeholder="login"/>
    <input type="password" placeholder="password"/>
    <input type="submit" />
</form>
```

In a browser, it will appear like the following:

Let's change the structure a little bit with wrapping divs:

```
<form>
    <div class="loginWrapper">
        <input type="text" placeholder="login"/>
    </div>
    <div class="passwordWrapper">
        <input type="password" placeholder="password"/>
    </div>
    <div class="submitWrapper">
        <input type="submit" />
    </div>
</form>
```

Now we have a base code to start styling:

Now we can start creating styles:

SASS:

```
*
box-sizing: border-box

form
width: 300px

input
margin-bottom: 5px
width: 100%

input[type="text"]
  border: 2px solid blue

input[type="password"]
  border: 2px solid green

input[type="submit"]
  background: #000
color: #fff
width: 100%
```

Generated CSS:

```
* {
    box-sizing: border-box;
}

form {
    width: 300px;
}

input {
```

```
        margin-bottom: 5px;
        width: 100%;
}

input[type="text"] {
        border: 2px solid blue;
}

input[type="password"] {
        border: 2px solid green;
}

input[type="submit"] {
        background: #000;
        color: #fff;
        width: 100%;
}
```

Now, after getting knowledge about proper selectors and adding basic CSS, our form looks like the following:

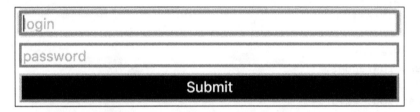

Let's look at the **Submit** button. We need to remove its border. In this iteration, let's add some pseudoelements. Let's update our SASS code as follows:

```
=ring($size, $color, $width)
  width: $size
height: $size
border-radius: 50%
  border: $width solid $color
background: none


=triangleRight($width, $height, $color)
  width: 0
  height: 0
  border-style: solid
  border-width: $height/2 0 $height/2 $width
```

```
     border-color: transparent transparent transparent $color

*
  box-sizing: border-box

form
  width: 300px

input
  margin-bottom: 5px
  width: 100%

input[type="text"]
  border: 2px solid blue

input[type="password"]
  border: 2px solid green

input[type="submit"]
  background: #000
  color: #fff
  width: 100%

.loginWrapper,
.passwordWrapper,
.submitWrapper
  position: relative

  &:after
    content: ''
    display: inline-block
    position: absolute
    top: 50%
    right: 10px

.loginWrapper,
.passwordWrapper
  &:after
    margin-top: -6px
    right: 10px
    +ring(4px, #000, 2px)

.submitWrapper
  &:after
```

```
    margin-top: -3px
    right: 10px
    +triangleRight(6px, 6px, #fff)
```

Generated CSS:

```
* {
    box-sizing: border-box;
}

form {
    width: 300px;
}

input {
    margin-bottom: 5px;
    width: 100%;
}

input[type="text"] {
    border: 2px solid blue;
}

input[type="password"] {
    border: 2px solid green;
}

input[type="submit"] {
    background: #000;
    color: #fff;
    width: 100%;
}

.loginWrapper,
.passwordWrapper,
.submitWrapper {
    position: relative;
}

.loginWrapper:after,
.passwordWrapper:after,
.submitWrapper:after {
    content: "";
    display: inline-block;
    position: absolute;
```

```
    top: 50%;
    right: 10px;
}

.loginWrapper:after,
.passwordWrapper:after {
    margin-top: -6px;
    right: 10px;
    width: 4px;
    height: 4px;
    border-radius: 50%;
    border: 2px solid #000;
    background: none;
}

.submitWrapper:after {
    margin-top: -3px;
    right: 10px;
    width: 0;
    height: 0;
    border-style: solid;
    border-width: 3px 0 3px 6px;
    border-color: transparent transparent transparent #fff;
}
```

The resulting output is as follows:

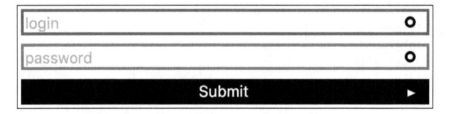

As we can see, we omitted the problem with `:before` and `:after` pseudoelements.

Don't forget about placeholders

With HTML5, we have a support in all browsers' placeholder attribute. It gives us an opportunity to add a description of the following:

```
::-webkit-input-placeholder
  color: red


::-moz-placeholder
```

```
    color: red

::-ms-input-placeholder
    color: red
```

Compiled CSS:

```
::-webkit-input-placeholder {
    color: red;
}

::-moz-placeholder {
    color: red;
}

::-ms-input-placeholder {
    color: red;
}
```

The resulting output is as follows:

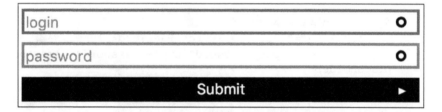

Complex form based on input[type="text"] and labels

So let's start with the styling of complex and elastic forms. Let's assume that we need to create a form with labels and inputs, where labels are always on the left and inputs are resizing. Let's bring the HTML structure:

```
<form class="" action="index.html" method="post">
    <fieldset>
        <legend>Personal data</legend>

        <div class="fieldKeeper">
            <label for="input_name">Your name</label>
            <input id="input_name" type="text" name="name" value="">
        </div>
```

```
            <div class="fieldKeeper">
                <label for="input_surname">Your surname</label>
                <input id="input_surname" type="text" name="name"
    value="">
            </div>

            <div class="fieldKeeper">
                <label for="input_address">Address</label>
                <input id="input_address" type="text" name="name"
    value="">
            </div>
        </fieldset>

        <fieldset>
            <legend>Login data</legend>
            <div class="fieldKeeper">
                <label for="input_login">Login</label>
                <input id="input_login" type="text" name="name" value=""
    placeholder="Your login">
            </div>

            <div class="fieldKeeper">
                <label for="input_password">Password</label>
                <input id="input_password" type="password" name="password"
    value="" placeholder="Password">
            </div>

            <div class="fieldKeeper">
                <label for="input_password_confirm">Confirm password</
    label>
                <input id="input_password_confirm" type="password"
    name="confirm_password" value="" placeholder="Confirmed password">
            </div>
        </fieldset>
    </form>
```

The preceding code will look like the following in a browser:

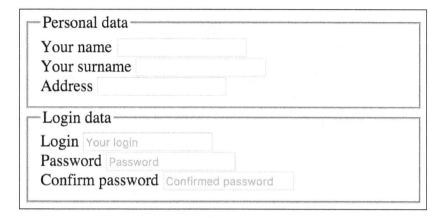

As you can see, it now behaves almost like it should but its inputs are not in 100% of width. When you change it to 100%, the label will be moved over the input. So what we can do is to wrap the input in an additional div and use a trick with padding and position absolute/relative. Let's change our HTML code into first fieldset:

```
<fieldset>
    <legend>Login data</legend>
    <div class="fieldKeeper">
        <label for="input_login">Login</label>
        <div class="inputKeeper">
            <input id="input_login" type="text" name="name" value=""
placeholder="Your login">
        </div>
    </div>

    <div class="fieldKeeper">
        <label for="input_password">Password</label>
        <div class="inputKeeper">
            <input id="input_password" type="password" name="password"
value="" placeholder="Password">
        </div>
    </div>

    <div class="fieldKeeper">
        <label for="input_password_confirm">Confirm password</label>
        <div class="inputKeeper">
            <input id="input_password_confirm" type="password"
name="confirm_password" value=""
```

```
                    placeholder="Confirmed password">
          </div>
        </div>
</fieldset>
```

After this change in the first `fieldset` only, you will see how the code behaves with and without an additional `inputKeeper` div. Let's use the following SASS code:

```
.fieldKeeper
  position: relative

fieldset
  width: auto
  border: 2px solid green

legend
  text-transform: uppercase
  font:
    size: 10px
    weight: bold

label
  position: absolute
  width: 200px
  display: inline-block
  left: 0
  font:
    size: 12px

.inputKeeper
  padding:
    left: 200px

input
  width: 100%
```

Compiled CSS:

```
.fieldKeeper {
    position: relative;
}

fieldset {
    width: auto;
    border: 2px solid green;
```

```
    }

legend {
    text-transform: uppercase;
    font-size: 10px;
    font-weight: bold;
}

label {
    position: absolute;
    width: 200px;
    display: inline-block;
    left: 0;
    font-size: 12px;
}

.inputKeeper {
    padding-left: 200px;
}

input {
    width: 100%;
}
```

Now what you can see in the browser is as follows:

And on a bigger screen, you will see the following:

As we can see, position absolute for label without an additional wrapper caused the problem with overlaying the label over the input. An additional wrapper gives us an opportunity to add a padding. In place of this padding, we can push a label with position absolute. After appending wrappers to the second section, it should look in the browser like the following:

How to style textarea

Styling of `textarea` is pretty simple and very comparable to the styling of text input. One of the differences is the opportunity to resize `textarea`. This is same as the `input[type="text"]` textarea which can have a placeholder so that you can add a styling for it. Let's prepare simple HTML code for short investigation about textarea:

```
<textarea placeholder="Here describe your skills"></textarea>
```

Now in the browser, you will see the following:

Remember not to add any space or end of line in between the opening and closing tags because it will be treated as a content of `textarea`. This will cause a problem with the placeholder.

And SASS code:

```
textarea
  width: 300px
  height: 150px
  resize: none
  border: 2px solid green
```

Compiled CSS:

```
textarea {
    width: 300px;
    height: 150px;
    resize: none;
    border: 2px solid green;
}
```

In the browser, you will see the following:

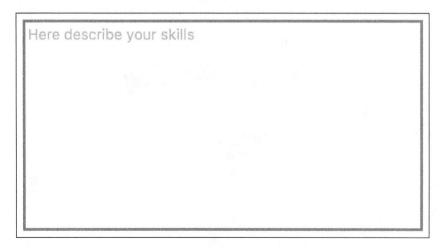

As values of property resize, you can use the following ones:

- `none`: This disables resizement in both axes
- `vertical`: This enables vertical resizement and blocks horizontal resizement
- `horizontal`: This enables horizontal resizement and blocks vertical resizement
- `both`: This enables resizement in both axes

Styling of select (drop down)

Hell yeah... the styling of `select` (drop down) is not as simple as it should be. In most cases, you will need to use some JavaScript plugin to make it easier. But what can you do with the simple CSS/HTML code? Let's get the following code:

```
<select>
    <option>Please choose one option...</option>
    <option>Option one</option>
    <option>Option two</option>
    <option>Option three</option>
    <option>Option four</option>
    <option>Option five</option>
</select>
```

The preceding code will generate an unstyled select box like the following:

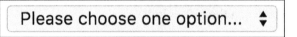

And after focus action, it gives the following output:

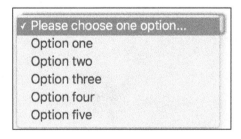

What can we do with it now? Let's try to add more flavor. Firstly, let's wrap it into additional elements:

```html
<div class="selectWrapper">
    <select>
        <option>Please choose one option...</option>
        <option>Option one</option>
        <option>Option two</option>
        <option>Option three</option>
        <option>Option four</option>
        <option>Option five</option>
    </select>
</div>
```

Now let's add an SASS code:

```sass
=triangleBottom($width, $height, $color)
  width: 0
  height: 0
  border-style: solid
  border-width: $height $width/2 0 $width/2
  border-color: $color transparent transparent transparent

.selectWrapper
  width: 300px
  border: 2px solid green
  overflow: hidden
  position: relative

  &:after
    content: ''
    position: absolute
    +triangleBottom(10px, 6px, red)
    right: 5px
    margin-top: -3px
    top: 50%

select
  background: #fff
  color: black
  font:
    size: 14px
  border: none
  width: 105%
```

Compiled CSS:

```
.selectWrapper {
    width: 300px;
    border: 2px solid green;
    overflow: hidden;
    position: relative;
}

.selectWrapper:after {
    content: "";
    position: absolute;
    width: 0;
    height: 0;
    border-style: solid;
    border-width: 6px 5px 0 5px;
    border-color: red transparent transparent transparent;
    right: 5px;
    margin-top: -3px;
    top: 50%;
}

select {
    background: #fff;
    color: black;
    font-size: 14px;
    border: none;
    width: 105%;
}
```

Please choose one option...   ▼

As you can see, this approach is pretty tricky. We made select a little bit wider than the container to move the native controls out. Then we added an overflow hidden to container. Additionally, we added the after element to add a triangle.

Summary

In this chapter, you gained knowledge about styling forms. It's pretty tricky to deal with all of them but as you can see there is always some solution (for example, with additional wrappers) to do that. I recommend you to create a simple framework with which you can deal with forms. It makes you fully prepared to style forms.

In the next chapter, we will try to resolve the most repeatable classic problems with CSS, such as the centering of elements, dealing with display types and many more. It will be a show of old school and new school methodologies possible with new CSS features.

7
Resolving Classic Problems

As a frontend developer, you are always dealing with classic CSS problems. The most known and repeatable issues are centering elements in both axes and opacity. With current CSS, you can do it pretty simple, but you need to have a foundation to know how to do it. Knowledge about fallbacks of previous versions of browsers can be used in some other further techniques. That's why they are added to this chapter.

In this chapter, we will:

- Learn how to center elements in both axes
- Learn how to deal with opacity
- Gather both the preceding tricks and create an effect similar to the trendy lightbox effect

Centering elements

Centering elements is an aspect known since the first CSS versions. There were always some element/elements on a page that needed to be centered vertically or horizontally in some container or in a browser. The easiest way to center some elements was to append the element into a table element and add to it vertical align and horizontal align attributes in HTML:

```
<td valign="middle" align="center>  </td>
```

But how can we do this in modern CSS? There are two kinds of centering:

- Horizontal
- Vertical

Let's resolve this problem.

Inline elements – horizontal centering

Let's assume that we have a text that we need to center. It is very simple. We just need to add `text-align: center` and that's it. In the example that we will implement, the background for our container is set to `red` and the element's background is set to `white` to see how it works.

Let's start with this HTML code:

```
<p class="container">
    <span class="element">Centered</span>
</p>
```

And SASS code:

```
.container
  background: red
  padding: 20px

.element
  background: white
```

CSS:

```
.container {
    background: red;
    padding: 20px;
}

.element {
    background: white;
}
```

What we will see in browser is as follows:

To center the box, as mentioned previously, we need to add `text-align: center` to the container:

SASS:

```
.container
  text-align: center
  background: red
  padding: 20px

.element
  background: white
```

Now in the browser, we can see the following:

Let's assume that we have both block elements and we want to adjust them as in the preceding example. What do we need to do? We need to change the display type to `inline` or `inline-block`. Let's change the HTML code a little bit:

```
<div class="container">
    <div class="element">Centered</div>
</div>
```

Now with the SASS code added previously, our example will behave similar to the following screenshot:

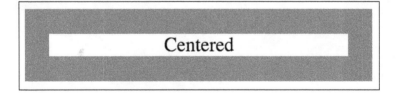

As we can see in the preceding screenshot, the block element is taking the full possible weight. What we need to do is to modify the SASS code:

```
.container
  text-align: center
  background: red
  padding: 20px

.element
```

```
    background: white
    display: inline-block
```

CSS:

```css
.container {
    text-align: center;
    background: red;
    padding: 20px;
}

.element {
    background: white;
    display: inline-block;
}
```

Now in the browser, we can see the following:

Block elements – centering in both axes

Let's start with the code from the previous chapter, which will be the base for our CSS styling. This is the element in `container`:

```html
<div class="container">
    <div class="element">Centered</div>
</div>
```

The SASS code with colors is added for better visibility of the problems:

```
.container
  background: black

.element
  width: 400px
  height: 400px
  background: red
```

CSS:

```css
.container {
    background: black;
}

.element {
    width: 400px;
    height: 400px;
    background: red;
}
```

In the starting point, our code in the browser will like the following:

As we can see in the preceding screenshot, our container with `Centered` content is now on the left side of black container. Let's assume that this is the container for the page that needs to be centered and stuck to the top of the page:

```
.container
  background: black
  height: 800px

.element
  width: 400px
  height: 400px
  background: red
  margin: 0 auto
```

Compiled:

```
.container {
    background: black;
    height: 800px;
}

.element {
    width: 400px;
    height: 400px;
    background: red;
    margin: 0 auto;
}
```

The most important line is the one in bold. This makes our container centered, as shown in the following screenshot:

So what can we do to center it in both axes? The old school way, with the known width and height of the element, is to add the container relative position to the element absolute position. The element needs to be moved from the top and left by 50%. Then we need to shift the element with a half of the known height to the top and left side using negative margins:

```
.container
  position: relative

.element
  position: absolute
  width: 100px
  height: 100px
  left: 50%
  right: 50%
  margin-left: -50px
  margin-top: -50px
```

CSS:

```css
.container {
    position: relative;
}

.element {
    position: absolute;
    width: 100px;
    height: 100px;
    left: 50%;
    right: 50%;
    margin-left: -50px;
    margin-top: -50px;
}
```

The output will be as follows:

As you can see in the preceding screenshot, the element is centered in both axes. The biggest issue is the static width and height of the element. Yes, of course, there is a way to add a JavaScript code to achieve it, but it's better to use native CSS functions. So let's try to make it with the `transform` property.

Using transform in centering

In the previous section, we have been trying to resolve the problem of centering elements. Let's extend it with the transform declaration. We will dig deeper into transform in the next chapter to understand how it works with rotation and scale, but for this chapter, we need to add the following code:

```
.container
  position: relative

.element
  position: absolute
  left: 50%
  right: 50%
  transform: translate(-50%, -50%)
```

The last line in the preceding code is making the same effect as it did in the previous section, defining the negative left and top margins. The best feature of this code is that we can add it everywhere without knowledge of the width and height. In the next chapter, we will learn about flexbox, which can be used for the centering of elements.

Dealing with opacity

Opacity occurs in projects very often. For example, when you are creating some model windows on a page or lightbox-like gallery. It is used on the layer added under the main window (overlay element), which, in most cases, has added an `onclick` event listener in JavaScript, which hides the window upon clicking. How can you create this effect? How was it done in the past? Let's start with a simple HTML code:

```
<header> Header </header>
<main> Lorem ipsum dolor sit amet, consectetur adipisicing elit.
Architecto dolore doloremque dolores iure laudantium magni mollitia
quam ratione, temporibus ut? Aperiam necessitatibus perspiciatis qui
ratione vel! Adipisci eligendi sint unde. </main>
<footer> Footer </footer>
```

SASS:

```
header, footer, main
  padding: 50px
  text-align: center

header, footer
  background: red

main
  background: green
```

Compiled:

```
header, footer, main {
    padding: 50px;
    text-align: center;
}

header, footer {
    background: red;
}

main {
    background: green;
}
```

Now it will look like the following:

What we need to do is to add a layer with opacity over the actually visible container. Let's append this code after the currently added code:

```
<div class="window_container">
    <div class="window">Content of our window</div>
</div>
```

What we need to do now is to change the container position to `fixed` and change the position of the element to `absolute`. Let's add a little bit more code to add more styling for better visibility of effects of our work:

```
.window_container
  position: fixed
  width: 100%
  height: 100%
  top: 0
  left: 0
  background: black

.window
  position: absolute
  width: 200px
  height: 200px
  background: white
  top: 50%
  left: 50%
  -webkit-transform: translate(-50%, -50%)
  -moz-transform: translate(-50%, -50%)
  -ms-transform: translate(-50%, -50%)
  -o-transform: translate(-50%, -50%)
  transform: translate(-50%, -50%)
```

Compiled:

```
.window_container {
    position: fixed;
    width: 100%;
    height: 100%;
    top: 0;
    left: 0;
    background: black;
}

.window {
    position: absolute;
    width: 200px;
```

```
        height: 200px;
        background: white;
        top: 50%;
        left: 50%;
        -webkit-transform: translate(-50%, -50%);
        -moz-transform: translate(-50%, -50%);
        -ms-transform: translate(-50%, -50%);
        -o-transform: translate(-50%, -50%);
        transform: translate(-50%, -50%);
    }
```

In the browser, we will see the white centered block on a black container as follows:

The preceding code is going to be the base in the next section, where we will see the differences between opacity and rgba.

Opacity versus RGBA – differences and where can we use them

Let's try to make the .window_container element added previously into the HTML/SASS structure be transparent. The easiest way to do it is add opacity: .5. So let's try to add the following code to our current SASS code:

```
.window_container
  opacity: .5
  position: fixed
  width: 100%
  height: 100%
  top: 0
  left: 0
  background: black
```

CSS:

```
.window_container {
    opacity: 0.5;
    position: fixed;
    width: 100%;
    height: 100%;
    top: 0;
    left: 0;
    background: black;
}
```

The effect in browser will be as shown in the following screenshot:

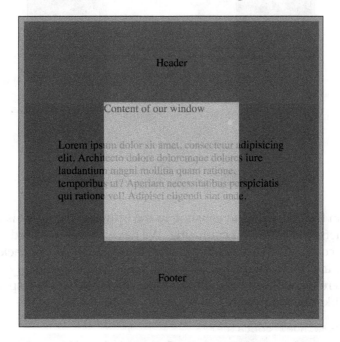

As we can see in the preceding screenshot, opacity is inherited by the element inside our `.window_container`. It's not the way we want to have it, so we have to change the CSS (SASS) or HTML code. If we want to change the HTML code, we can do it this way:

```
<div class="window_container"> </div>
<div class="window">Content of our window</div>
```

And the SASS code will be changed in the window description. We will change only the position to `fixed`:

```
.window
  position: fixed
```

The effect in the browser will be as follows:

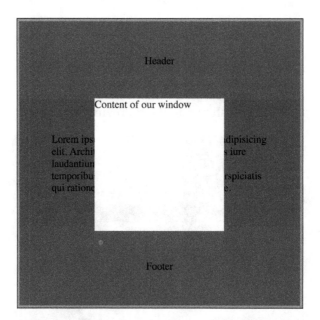

As we can see in the preceding screenshot, in the browser, the effect is achieved but our HTML structure is a little bit confusing. We have parallely added two elements into the HTML code, which are related to one element. So let's get back to the code from the beginning of our chapter where `.window` is in the `.window_container`. This is the place where we will use `rgba`. Be sure that the HTML code responsible for the window looks like the following:

```
<div class="window_container">
    <div class="window">Content of our window</div>
</div>
```

What we need to do is to change the definition of the background color of the window_container and append our rgba. As we know, we can define colors of elements in few ways:

- Adding color names (black, white, red, ...)
- Hex colors definition (#ff00ff, #fff ...)
- RGB (rgb(0,0,0), rgb(255,255,255)) based on R(ed)G(reen)B(lue)
- HSL (hsl(100, 90%, 50%)) based on H(ue) S(aturation) L(ightness)
- RGBA (rgb(0,0,0, .4), rgb(255,255,255, .7)) based on R(ed)G(reen) B(lue) + alpha channel
- HSLA (hsl(100, 90%, 50%, .8)) based on H(ue) S(aturation) L(ightness) + alpha channel

In our case, we will use rgba. The final SASS code for window_container is as follows:

```
.window_container
  position: fixed
  width: 100%
  height: 100%
  top: 0
  left: 0
  background: rgba(0,0,0,.5)

.window
  position: fixed
  width: 200px
  height: 200px
  background: white
  top: 50%
  left: 50%
  -webkit-transform: translate(-50%, -50%)
  -moz-transform: translate(-50%, -50%)
  -ms-transform: translate(-50%, -50%)
  -o-transform: translate(-50%, -50%)
  transform: translate(-50%, -50%)
```

Compiled:

```
.window_container {
    position: fixed;
    width: 100%;
    height: 100%;
    top: 0;
    left: 0;
```

```
        background: rgba(0, 0, 0, 0.5);
    }

    .window {
        position: fixed;
        width: 200px;
        height: 200px;
        background: white;
        top: 50%;
        left: 50%;
        -webkit-transform: translate(-50%, -50%);
        -moz-transform: translate(-50%, -50%);
        -ms-transform: translate(-50%, -50%);
        -o-transform: translate(-50%, -50%);
        transform: translate(-50%, -50%);
    }
```

As you can see, the `opacity` declaration is removed. Color is defined as RGBA. The rest of code is the same. The code in the browser will look like the following:

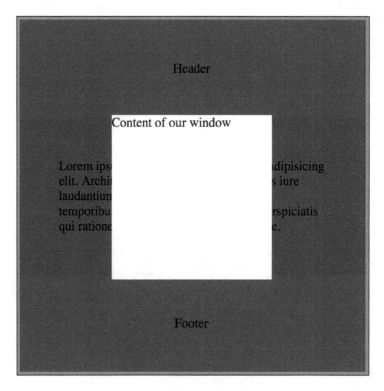

Opacity in the past – fallback for old IE versions

Fallback for old browsers was done in a similar way as it was when you wanted to use border radius—you needed to use images. How was it finally done? When the graphics were cut in graphic software, the overlay was cut as a small transparent image, for example, PNG 1px per 1px. Then it was added as a background and repeated in *x* and *y* axes.

```
/* FALLBACK */
.window_container
  background-image: url(<1x1.png>)
  background-repeat: repeat
```

Summary

In this chapter, you gained knowledge about the most known, classic issues in CSS: centering and opacity. You resolved this problem and gained knowledge about the pros and cons of the solutions. Additionally, you learned how the opacity problem was resolved in old browsers.

In the next chapter, you will learn about modern CSS aspects like flexbox gradients, shadows, transforms, and data attributes. You will also learn about some tricks that you can apply to your code using this feature. Let's move on to the next chapter.

8

Usage of Flexbox Transform

CSS is still developing. Each year, as a frontend developer, you need to watch current trends and new properties that you can set for the elements. Of course, there is a bunch of restrictions, but in some cases, those restrictions don't exist, for example, in new browsers or selected mobile apps or because of set requirements. In this chapter, we will cover the following topics:

- Flexbox
- Transform properties

Flexbox

Flexbox is the one of the loudest and most modern layout methodologies used in current CSS projects. With flexbox, you can create a structure for your web page, which is more elastic than projects based on floating boxes. Why? We will check and make an investigation in this chapter. What you need to remember is that Internet Explorer supports flexbox since its 11th version.

Let's look at the basics of flexbox:

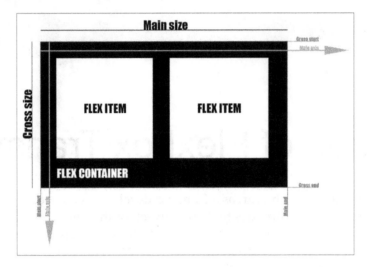

As you can see in the preceding screenshot, there is new dictionary related to flexbox:

- **Main axis** (green arrow)
- **Main start** (red line)
- **Main end** (red line)
- **Main size** (black line)
- **Cross axis** (green arrow)
- **Cross start** (red line)
- **Cross end** (red line)
- **Cross size** (black line)

Initialization of flexbox is very simple. You just need to add the following code to your container:

```
.flexContainer
  display: -webkit-box
  display: -moz-box
  display: -ms-flexbox
  display: -webkit-flex
  display: flex
```

The compiled code is:

```
.flexContainer {

    display: -webkit-box;

    display: -moz-box;

    display: -ms-flexbox;

    display: -webkit-flex;

    display: flex;

}
```

The usage of flexbox still needs prefixes for cross-browser compatibility. This is a good reason to create reusable mixins:

```
=displayFlex

  display: -webkit-box

  display: -moz-box

  display: -ms-flexbox

  display: -webkit-flex

  display: flex
```

Now we can create the same `.flexContainer` like the following:

```
.flexContainer

  +displayFlex
```

The compiled code is:

```
.flexContainer {
    display: -webkit-box;
    display: -moz-box;
    display: -ms-flexbox;
    display: -webkit-flex;
    display: flex;

}
```

Let's create a few elements within the container:

```
<div class="flexContainer">

    <div class="flexElement">Element 1</div>

    <div class="flexElement">Element 2</div>

    <div class="flexElement">Element 3</div>

</div>
```

And let's decorate a little bit our CSS code to see how the flexbox behaves:

```
=displayFlex

  display: -webkit-box

  display: -moz-box

  display: -ms-flexbox

  display: -webkit-flex

  display: flex


.flexContainer

  +displayFlex

  background: red
```

The compiled code is:

```
.flexContainer {

    display: -webkit-box;

    display: -moz-box;

    display: -ms-flexbox;

    display: -webkit-flex;

    display: flex;

    background: red;

}
```

Now we will see in the browser the following view:

Element 1Element 2Element 3

You can see from the preceding screenshot that the container is not reaching the full possible height in the browser, but it does reach its full width. Inside the elements are floated to the left side. Now let's change the SASS code a little bit:

```
.flexContainer

  +displayFlex

  height: 100%

  background: red

.blue

  background: blue

.green

  background: green

.yellow

  background: yellow
```

The compiled code is:

```
.flexContainer {

    display: -webkit-box;

    display: -moz-box;

    display: -ms-flexbox;

    display: -webkit-flex;

    display: flex;
```

```
        height: 100%;

        background: red;

    }

    .blue {

        background: blue;

    }

    .green {

        background: green;

    }

    .yellow {

        background: yellow;

    }
```

And let's add a color class to our HTML code:

```
<div class="flexContainer">

    <div class="flexElement blue">Element 1</div>

    <div class="flexElement green">Element 2</div>

    <div class="flexElement yellow">Element 3</div>

</div>
```

And in the browser, you will see the following:

As you can see in the preceding screenshot, the container has a full width and height, and inside the elements are behaving like inline elements but with the full height inherited from the container. This is because of the property called align-item, whose default value is **stretch**. Let's dig a little bit more into the values of this property.

Flexbox property align-items

This is one of the properties that we can add to flexContainer. It has a few values that we can set. For now, we know how the default stretch value behaves. Let's study the rest of the possible values. Before all the values, let's change HTML and CSS code a little bit to see better all the behaviors.

Let's modify the HTML code as follows:

```
<div class="flexContainer">

    <div class="flexElement blue h200px">Element 1</div>

    <div class="flexElement green h300px">Element 2</div>

    <div class="flexElement yellow h100px">Element 3</div>

</div>
```

Let's append the following SASS code:

```
.h100px

  height: 100px

.h200px

  height: 200px

.h300px

  height: 300px
```

The CSS file is:

```
.h100px {

    height: 100px;

}

.h200px {

    height: 200px;

}

.h300px {

    height: 300px;

}
```

Different values of flex that can be used are as follows:

- `stretch` (default)

 For this value stretch, you need to remove classes that are adding the height of boxes (h100px, h200px, h300px).

- flex-start

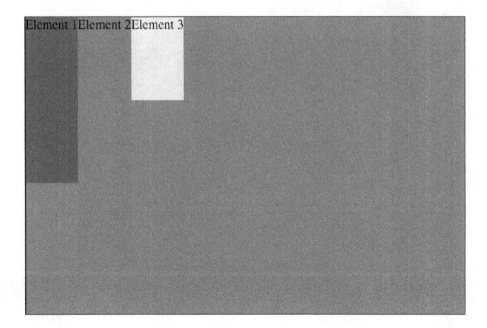

- `flex-end`

- `center`

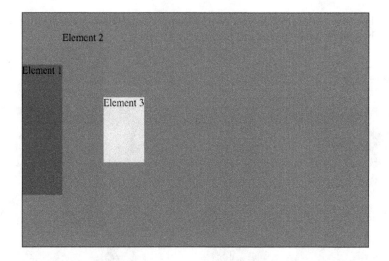

- `baseline`

In this case, for a better understanding of this behavior, let's change our code to see how the baseline is designated:

```html
<div class="flexContainer">
    <div class="flexElement blue h200px">Element 1</div>
    <div class="flexElement green h300px">Element 2 Lorem ipsum dolor
sit amet, consectetur adipisicing elit. Possimus necessitatibus est
quis sequi, sapiente quos corporis, dignissimos libero quibusdam
beatae ipsam quaerat? Excepturi magni voluptas dicta inventore
necessitatibus omnis officia.</div>
    <div class="flexElement yellow h100px">Element 3</div>
</div>
```

And in SASS the code can be written as:

```
.h100px
  height: 100px
  font-size: 30px
  margin-top: 20px


.h200px
  height: 200px
  font-size: 20px


.h300px
  height: 300px
  font-size: 8px
```

The CSS code will be:

```css
.h100px {
    height: 100px;
    font-size: 30px;
    margin-top: 20px;
}


.h200px {
    height: 200px;
    font-size: 20px;
}


.h300px {
    height: 300px;
    font-size: 8px;
}
```

The output of the preceding code is as follows:

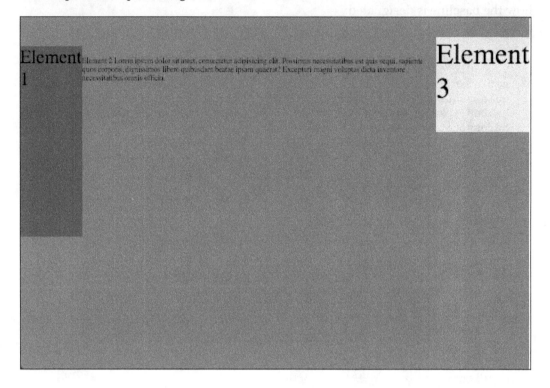

The position of the box from the top is set from the baseline designated by first line of text in the box. Purposeful there is added a margin-top for box described as h100px box to see that the baseline is counted for from any of the boxes in the set of children.

Okay. But how this example will behave when we will add a box without a text content? Let's modify HTML code as follows:

```html
<div class="flexContainer">
    <div class="flexElement blue h200px">Element 1</div>
    <div class="flexElement yellow h100px w100px"></div>
    <div class="flexElement green h300px">Element 2 Lorem ipsum dolor
sit amet, consectetur adipisicing elit. Possimus necessitatibus est
quis sequi, sapiente quos corporis, dignissimos libero quibusdam
beatae ipsam quaerat? Excepturi magni voluptas dicta inventore
necessitatibus omnis officia.</div>
    <div class="flexElement yellow h100px">Element 3</div>
</div>
```

And let's add the `w100px` class in SASS code:

```
.w100px
  width: 100px
```

```
CSS:
.w100px {
    width: 100px;
}
```

The output of the preceding code is as follows:

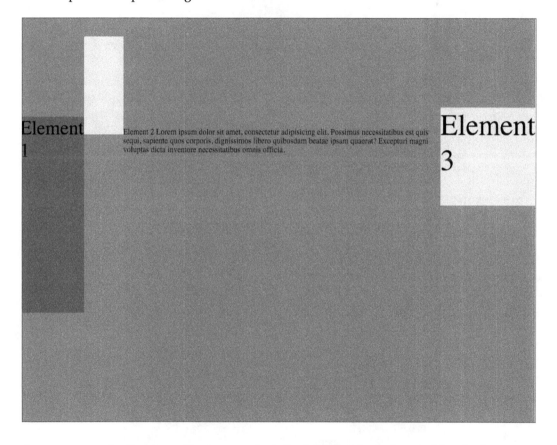

As we can see in the preceding screenshot, the baseline is designated by the bottom line of the yellow empty box.

Flexbox property flex-wrap

One of the next properties that we can set for the flex container is `flex-wrap`. This property is related to wrapping in the box. We can set `nowrap`, `wrap`, and `wrap-reverse` as values. How do they behave?

- `nowrap` (default)

- `wrap`

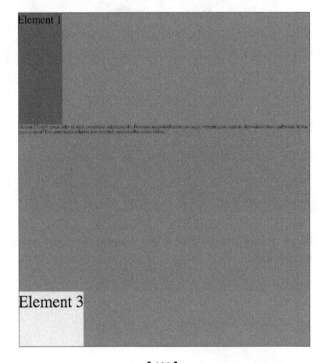

- `wrap-reverse`

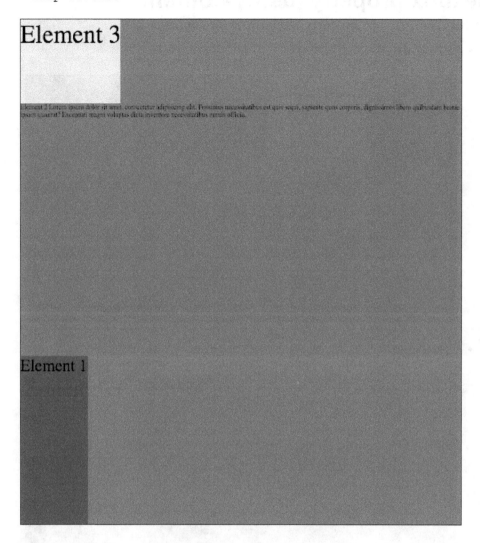

As you can see, `wrap` and `wrap-reverse` work in the same way but with one simple difference: `wrap-reverse` is changing the order of flex items.

Flexbox property justify-content

The justify-content property is related to the container too:

- flex-start

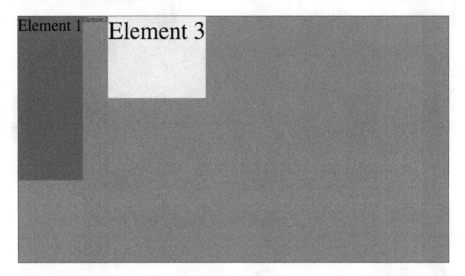

- flex-end

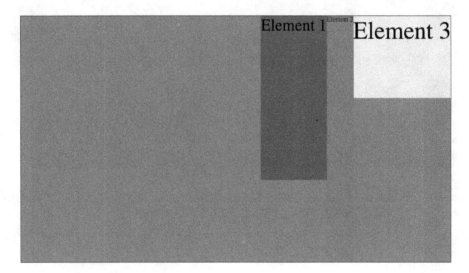

- center

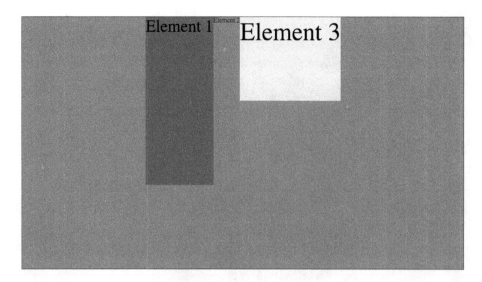

- space-between

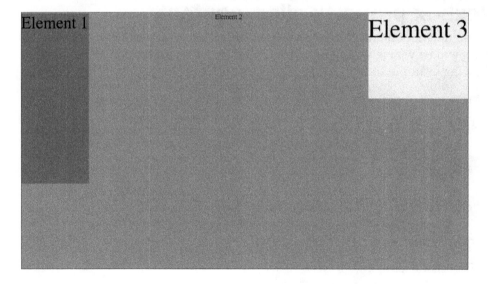

- `space-around`

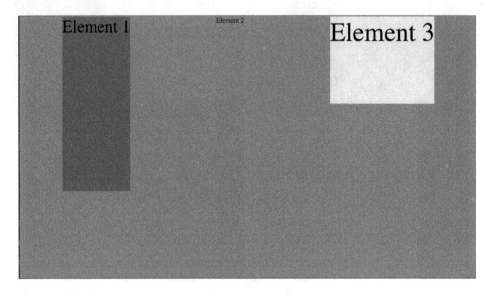

Flexbox property align-content

The alignment of items is related to `flexContainer`. You need to remember that the effects will be visible when you have at least two lines of items. So let's change the following example code:

HTML:

```
<div class="flexContainer">
    <div class="flexElement blue h100px">Element 1</div>
    <div class="flexElement green h200px">Element 2</div>
    <div class="flexElement blue h100px">Element 3</div>
    <div class="flexElement green h200px">Element 4</div>
    <div class="flexElement blue h100px">Element 5</div>
    <div class="flexElement green h200px">Element 6</div>
</div>
```

The SASS code is:

```
=displayFlex
  display: -webkit-box
  display: -moz-box
  display: -ms-flexbox
  display: -webkit-flex
  display: flex
```

```
.flexContainer
  height: 600px
  width: 900px
  +displayFlex
  flex-wrap: wrap
  background: red

.blue
  background: blue

.green
  background: green

.yellow
  background: yellow

.h100px
  height: 100px
  font-size: 30px
  margin-top: 20px

.h200px
  height: 200px
  font-size: 20px

.h300px
  height: 300px
  font-size: 8px


.w100px
  width: 100px

.flexElement
  width: 300px
```

The CSS code is:

```
.flexContainer {
    height: 600px;
    width: 900px;
    display: -webkit-box;
    display: -moz-box;
    display: -ms-flexbox;
    display: -webkit-flex;
```

```
        display: flex;
        flex-wrap: wrap;
        background: red;
}

.blue {
        background: blue;
}

.green {
        background: green;
}

.yellow {
        background: yellow;
}

.h100px {
        height: 100px;
        font-size: 30px;
        margin-top: 20px;
}

.h200px {
        height: 200px;
        font-size: 20px;
}

.h300px {
        height: 300px;
        font-size: 8px;
}

.w100px {
        width: 100px;
}

.flexElement {
        width: 300px;
}
```

- `flex-start`

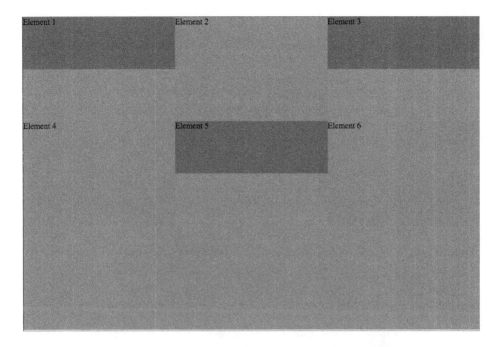

- `flex-end`

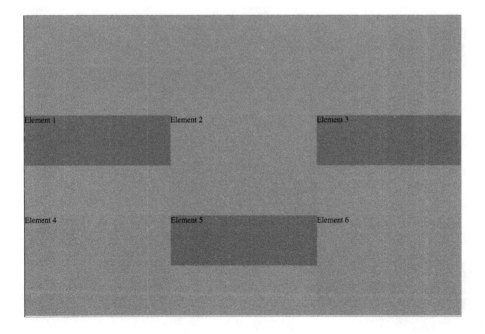

- center

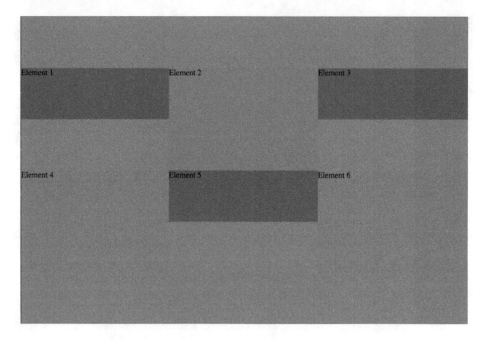

- space-between

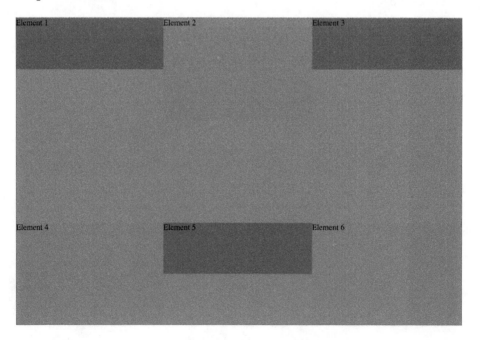

- space-around

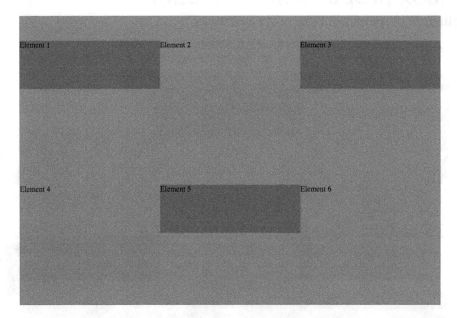

- stretch

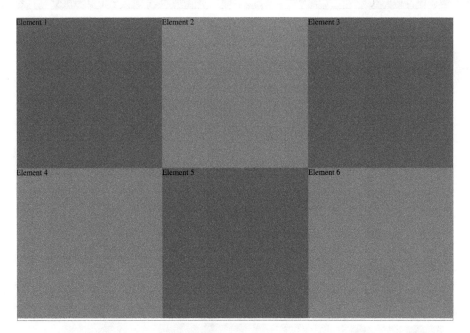

In the last example, all classes have been removed relating to height: h100px, h200px.

Flexbox property flex-direction

The different properties of flexbox are as follows:

- `row`

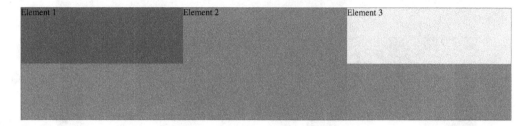

- `row-reverse`

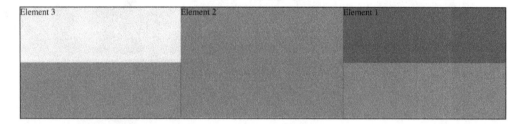

- `column`

- `column-reverse`

Useful mixins that you can add to your collection are as follows:

```
=displayFlex
  display: -webkit-box
  display: -moz-box
  display: -ms-flexbox
  display: -webkit-flex
  display: flex

=flexOrder($number)
  -webkit-box-ordinal-group: $number
  -moz-box-ordinal-group: $number
  -ms-flex-order: $number
  -webkit-order: $number
  order: $number
```

Usage of flexbox – creating page structure

When you are starting to work on a project, you are taking prepared layout as a graphic file and you need to make it available and interactive in the browser. Let's begin with the currently most known structure:

```
<div class="flexContainer">
    <header>Header</header>
    <aside>Side menu</aside>
    <main>Content</main>
    <footer>Footer - Copyright fedojo.com</footer>
</div>
```

So we want to take the header on the top aside from the left main on the right and footer on the bottom:

```
.flexContainer
  +displayFlex
  -webkit-flex-flow: row wrap
  flex-flow: row wrap


  & > *
     padding: 10px
     flex: 1 100%

  header
     background: red

  footer
     background: lightblue

  main
     background: yellow
     flex: 3 1 auto

  aside
     background: green
     flex:  0 0 auto
```

The CSS file is:

```
.flexContainer {
    display: -webkit-box;
    display: -moz-box;
    display: -ms-flexbox;
    display: -webkit-flex;
    display: flex;
    -webkit-flex-flow: row wrap;
    flex-flow: row wrap;
}

.flexContainer > * {
    padding: 10px;
    flex: 1 100%;
}
```

```
.flexContainer header {
    background: red;
}

.flexContainer footer {
    background: lightblue;
}

.flexContainer main {
    background: yellow;
    flex: 3 auto;
}

.flexContainer aside {
    background: green;
    flex: 1 auto;
}
```

The effect in browser will be as follows:

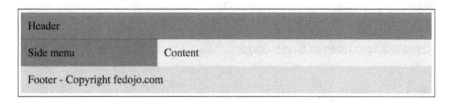

When you wish to change the sidebar width to a static value, you can append a small change into the SASS declaration of the side menu:

```
aside
  background: green
  flex:  0 0 auto
  width: 100px
```

And it will be in CSS:

```
.flexContainer aside {
    background: green;
    flex: 0 auto;
    width: 100px;
}
```

This will keep the left column static width.

Usage of flexbox – change order of boxes in mobile/tablet view

When you are creating HTML layout adjustment to a desktop and mobile, a few possibilities may occur where you need to change the order of the boxes. Easy examples for a desktop are as follows:

- First element needs to be on the top
- Second element needs to be on the bottom

Easy examples for a mobile are as follows:

- Second element needs to be on the top
- First element needs to be on the bottom

Let's use the following HTML code:

```
<div class="container">
    <div class="first">First</div>
    <div class="second">Second</div>
</div>
```

And let's create a few lines of SASS code:

```
=displayFlex
   display: -webkit-box
   display: -moz-box
   display: -ms-flexbox
   display: -webkit-flex
   display: flex

=flexOrder($number)
  -webkit-box-ordinal-group: $number
  -moz-box-ordinal-group: $number
  -ms-flex-order: $number
  -webkit-order: $number
  order: $number

.container > *
  padding: 20px

.first
  background: lightblue
```

```
.second
  background: lightcyan


@media screen and (max-width: 600px)

  .container
    +displayFlex
    -webkit-flex-flow: row wrap
    flex-flow: row wrap

    & > *
      width: 100%

    .first
      +flexOrder(2)

    .second
      +flexOrder(1)
```

In CSS:

```css
.container > * {
    padding: 20px;
}

.first {
    background: lightblue;
}

.second {
    background: lightcyan;
}

@media screen and (max-width: 600px) {
    .container {
        display: -webkit-box;
        display: -moz-box;
        display: -ms-flexbox;
        display: -webkit-flex;
        display: flex;
        -webkit-flex-flow: row wrap;
        flex-flow: row wrap;
    }
```

```
.container > * {
    width: 100%;
}

.container .first {
    -webkit-box-ordinal-group: 2;
    -moz-box-ordinal-group: 2;
    -ms-flex-order: 2;
    -webkit-order: 2;
    order: 2;
}

.container .second {
    -webkit-box-ordinal-group: 1;
    -moz-box-ordinal-group: 1;
    -ms-flex-order: 1;
    -webkit-order: 1;
    order: 1;
}
}
```

On the desktop, when the viewport width is wider than 600px, you can see the following:

And on a view smaller than 600px, you can see the following:

More about transform

Transformations are very useful for frontend developers because of basic graphic operations that you can perform using only CSS. In previous versions of CSS, it was only possible with JavaScript. In one of the previous chapters, we used `transform` for centering elements in the container. Let's now try to understand it more and check what else we can do with it:

The HTML file is:

```
<table>
    <tr>
        <td>no transform</td>
        <td><div class="transform_none">no transform</div></td>
    </tr>
    <tr>
        <td>rotate</td>
        <td><div class="transform_rotate">rotate</div></td>
        <td><div class="transform_rotatex">rotateX</div></td>
        <td><div class="transform_rotatey">rotateY</div></td>
        <td><div class="transform_rotatez">rotateZ</div></td>
    </tr>
    <tr>
        <td>skew</td>
        <td><div class="transform_skew">skew</div></td>
        <td><div class="transform_skewx">skewX</div></td>
        <td><div class="transform_skewy">skewY</div></td>
    </tr>
    <tr>
        <td>scale</td>
        <td><div class="transform_scale">scale</div></td>
        <td><div class="transform_scalex">scaleX</div></td>
        <td><div class="transform_scaley">scaleY</div></td>
        <td><div class="transform_scalez">scaleZ</div></td>
    </tr>
    <tr>
        <td>translate</td>
        <td><div class="transform_translate">translate</div></td>
        <td><div class="transform_translatex">translateX</div></td>
        <td><div class="transform_translatey">translateY</div></td>
        <td><div class="transform_translatez">translateZ</div></td>
    </tr>
    <tr>
        <td>multiple</td>
```

```
        <td><div class="transform_multiple01">multiple</div></td>
    </tr>

</table>
```

The SASS file is:

```
table
  border-collapse: collapse

  td, th
    border: 1px solid black


div[class^="transform_"]
  width: 100px
  height: 100px
  background: lightblue
  line-height: 100px
  text:
    align: center
    transform: uppercase
  font:
    weight: bold
    size: 10px
  display: inline-block

td
  text-align: center
  vertical-align: middle
  width: 150px
  height: 150px

.transform_
  /* Rotate */
  &rotate
    transform: rotate(25deg)

  &rotatex
    transform: rotateX(25deg)

  &rotatey
    transform: rotateY(25deg)
```

```
&rotatez
  transform: rotateZ(25deg)

/* Skew */
&skew
  transform: skew(10deg, 10deg)

&skewx
  transform: skewX(10deg)

&skewy
  transform: skewY(10deg)

/* Scale */
&scalex
  transform: scaleX(1.2)

&scale
  transform: scale(1.2)

&scaley
  transform: scaleY(1.2)

/* Translate */
&translate
  transform: translate(10px, 10px)

&translatex
  transform: translate(10%)

&translatey
  transform: translate(10%)

&translatez
  transform: translate(10%)

/* Multiple */
&multiple01
  transform: rotateX(25deg) translate(10px, 10px) skewX(10deg)
```

The CSS file is:

```css
table {
    border-collapse: collapse;
}

table td, table th {
    border: 1px solid black;
}

div[class^="transform_"] {
    width: 100px;
    height: 100px;
    background: lightblue;
    line-height: 100px;
    text-align: center;
    text-transform: uppercase;
    font-weight: bold;
    font-size: 10px;
    display: inline-block;
}

td {
    text-align: center;
    vertical-align: middle;
    width: 150px;
    height: 150px;
}

.transform_ {
    /* Rotate */
    /* Skew */
    /* Scale */
    /* Translate */
    /* Multiple */
}

.transform_rotate {
    transform: rotate(25deg);
}

.transform_rotatex {
    transform: rotateX(25deg);
}
```

```
.transform_rotatey {
    transform: rotateY(25deg);
}

.transform_rotatez {
    transform: rotateZ(25deg);
}

.transform_skew {
    transform: skew(10deg, 10deg);
}

.transform_skewx {
    transform: skewX(10deg);
}

.transform_skewy {
    transform: skewY(10deg);
}

.transform_scalex {
    transform: scaleX(1.2);
}

.transform_scale {
    transform: scale(1.2);
}

.transform_scaley {
    transform: scaleY(1.2);
}

.transform_translate {
    transform: translate(10px, 10px);
}

.transform_translatex {
    transform: translate(10%);
}

.transform_translatey {
    transform: translate(10%);
}
```

```
.transform_translatez {
    transform: translate(10%);
}

.transform_multiple01 {
    transform: rotateX(25deg) translate(10px, 10px) skewX(10deg);
}
```

The effect in the browser will be as follows:

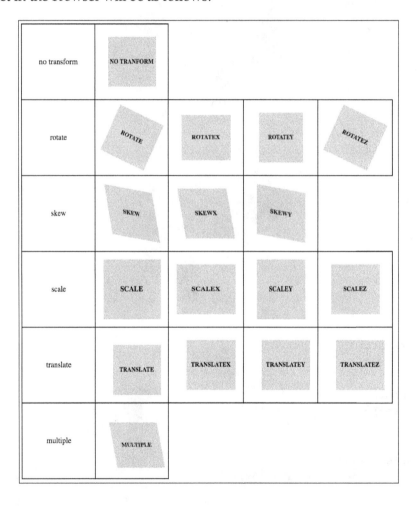

In the preceding example, there is a bunch of possible transforms in the sample view in the browser. In the first line, you can see the element without any transforms. In each of the next lines, you can check the following:

- **rotate**
- **skew**
- **scale**
- **translate**
- **multiple**

Important aspects of transforms are the units that can be used in each of the transform types:

- `rotate`: degrees, for example, `rotate(20deg, 40deg)`.
- `skew`: degrees, for example, `skew(30deg, 50deg)`.
- `scale`: number, where 1 = 100%, for example, `scale(1.5, 1.5)`.
- `translate`: units related to width, such as pixels percentages, for example, `translate(50%, 50%)`. Important information: percentages are related to the dimensions of the transformed object.

In the last line of the preceding screenshot, there is a sample which shows how transforms can be chained in one line. This sample can be used when you need to append more than one transform.

Summary

In this chapter, you gained knowledge about the main features of modern CSS. You learned how flexbox works and how you can use it in your projects. You analyzed two-dimensional transforms, which you can use in your projects. This chapter is an introduction to the new CSS features and will help you to understand possibilities.

In the next chapter, we will focus on gradients, shadows, and animations. We will create a linear and radial gradient box and text shadows, and additionally gain knowledge about the `calc` function.

9
Calc, Gradients, and Shadows

In the previous chapter, we analyzed flexbox and simple structures based on flexbox model. In this chapter, we will focus on the following aspects of CSS:

- Calc function
- Gradients
- Shadows
- CSS Animations.
- Usage of data-attribute

Let's begin!

The calc() method

Have you ever had a problem with mixing units? For example, say you needed to make an equation 60%-10px? These operations could be very helpful in old browsers and this is possible right now with the `calc()` method in CSS. How can you use it? Let's resolve a problem with two floating boxes; one has a static width and the second is adjusting to the possible max width. The code is as follows:

HTML:

```
<div class="container">
    <div class="first">First</div>
    <div class="second">Second</div>
</div>
```

SASS:

```
&:after
  content: ""
  display: table
  clear: both

.container
  +clearfix

  & > *
    float: left
    height: 200px
    padding: 10px
    box-sizing: border-box

  .first
    width: 100px
    background: red

  .second
    width: calc(100% - 100px)
    background: blue
```

Compiled CSS:

```
.container:after {
    content: "";
    display: table;
    clear: both;
}

.container >* {
    float: left;
    height: 200px;
    padding: 10px;
    box-sizing: border-box;
}

.first {
    width: 100px;
    background: red;
}
```

```
.second {
    width: calc(100% - 100px);
    background: blue;
}
```

Here's the end result:

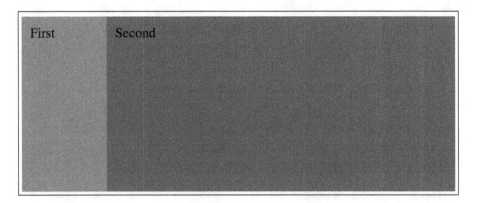

The `calc()` function gives us the opportunity to make simple equations such as percent minus pixels. In this simple example, you can see that we don't need to use tricks with paddings and absolute positions. You can use the `calc()` function in good way and the problem will be resolved.

Gradients in CSS

Experienced frontend developers remember the time when gradients were done as background images. Yes! That was the only idea to imitate gradients in browsers. You needed to cut 1px width and the gradient's height (if it was a vertical gradient; in the case of horizontal, it was 1px height and width was designated by the width of the gradient) from the PSD file. Then, you had to add it in CSS and repeat your *magic* image in the background.

Now, you can do it in CSS! Let's begin with linear gradients.

Linear gradients

Linear gradients can be of two types: from top-to-bottom or from left-to-right. Let's begin with a vertical gradient:

```
background: linear-gradient(to bottom, #000 0%, #f00 100%)
```

This code will generate a linear gradient from top-to-bottom. At the top, the color will be black and it will be red at the bottom.

However, it cannot be so easy to be a frontend developer. That's why you need to remember about prefixes:

```
background: -webkit-gradient(linear, left top, left bottom, color-
stop(0%, #000), color-stop(100%, #f00))
background: -moz-linear-gradient(top, #000 0%, #f00 100%)
background: -webkit-linear-gradient(top, #000 0%, #f00 100%)
background: -o-linear-gradient(top, #000 0%, #f00 100%)
background: -ms-linear-gradient(top, #000 0%, #f00 100%)
background: linear-gradient(to bottom, #000 0%, #f00 100%)
```

As you can see, the definition with prefixes takes up a lot of code, especially when you need a fallback for IE9 (the last line with the filter definition).

The basic horizontal gradient definition is as follows:

```
background: linear-gradient(left, #fff, #000)
```

This example will generate a gradient from left-to-right with white on the right and black on the left.

Here's the prefixed version:

```
background: -webkit-gradient(linear, left top, right top, from(#fff),
to(#000))
background: -webkit-linear-gradient(left, #fff, #000)
background: -moz-linear-gradient(left, #fff, #000)
```

```
background: -ms-linear-gradient(left, #fff, #000)
background: -o-linear-gradient(left, #fff, #000)
background: linear-gradient(left, #fff, #000)
```

What about multicolor gradients? Of course, it is possible:

```
background: linear-gradient(to right, black, red, white)
```

Here's the effect:

You can also rotate the gradient:

HTML:

```
<div class="gradient-04"></div>
```

SASS:

```
div[class^="gradient-"]
  height: 200px
  width: 200px
  margin-bottom: 20px


.gradient-04
  background: linear-gradient(45deg , black, red, white)
```

CSS:

```
div[class^="gradient-"] {
    height: 200px;
    width: 200px;
    margin-bottom: 20px;
}


.gradient-04 {
    background: linear-gradient(45deg, black, red, white);
}
```

Here's the effect in the browser:

What if you want to change the balance between colors? For example, maybe you want a higher concentration of black color in your gradient? This is also possible:

SASS:

```
.gradient-05
  background: linear-gradient(to right, black 40%, red 50%, white
100%)
```

CSS:

```
.gradient-05 {
    background: linear-gradient(to right, black 40%, red 50%, white
100%);
}
```

Here's the effect in the browser:

To understand this, you need to check this example step by step:

```
black 40%:This line means that black color will be finished in 40% of
width of the box
red 50%:This means that red color will be finished in 50% of width of
the box
white 100%:This means that white color will be finished in 100% of
width of the box
```

Using gradient mixins

In this chapter, you can get these mixins and use them in your projects. I don't like to write long code every time—just write it once and then repeat the short version. That's why I prepared these two simple gradients:

```
=linearGradientFromTop($startColor, $endColor)
  background: $startColor
  background: -webkit-gradient(linear, left top, left bottom, color-
stop(0%, $startColor), color-stop(100%, $endColor))
  background: -moz-linear-gradient(top, $startColor 0%, $endColor
100%)
  background: -webkit-linear-gradient(top, $startColor 0%, $endColor
100%)
  background: -o-linear-gradient(top, $startColor 0%, $endColor 100%)
  background: -ms-linear-gradient(top, $startColor 0%, $endColor100%)
  background: linear-gradient(to bottom, $startColor 0%, $endColor
100%)
  filter: progid:DXImageTransform.Microsoft.gradient(
startColorstr='#{$startColor}', endColorstr='#{$endColor}',GradientTy
pe=0 )

=linearGradientFromLeft($startColor, $endColor)
  background-color: $startColor
background: -webkit-gradient(linear, left top, right top,
from($startColor), to($endColor))
  background: -webkit-linear-gradient(left, $startColor, $endColor)
  background: -moz-linear-gradient(left, $startColor, $endColor)
  background: -ms-linear-gradient(left, $startColor, $endColor)
  background: -o-linear-gradient(left, $startColor, $endColor)
  background: linear-gradient(left, $startColor, $endColor)
  filter: progid:DXImageTransform.Microsoft.gradient(startColorStr='#{
$startColor}', endColorStr='#{$endColor}', gradientType='1')
```

One of the most important things in the preceding examples of mixins is that you need to use the full representation of hex colors. You can't use, for example, #f00 for red color. You have to use #ff0000. It's because of IE9 and lower fallback which does not respect this shorter version of color representation in gradients. Another important thing in this mixin is the first line, which sets only the background color. This is a fallback for all browsers that don't respect any prefixed/non-prefixed versions of gradients. With it the color is set only to the color which is set as a $startColor. The second line in the mixin is related to old versions of browsers based on WebKit. The last line relates to old IE (9 and lower). Of course, you don't have to keep this code in your projects if it's not used or not needed. You can modify it to match your project's requirements.

Radial gradients

In some projects, you will need to add radial gradients. The radial gradient standard function looks like this:

```
radial-gradient()
```

Or you can use:

```
background: repeating-radial-gradient()
```

Let's check an example code and the possibilities of gradients' usage:

HTML:

```
<table>
    <tr>
        <td><div class="gradient-04"></div></td>
        <td><div class="gradient-05"></div></td>
        <td><div class="gradient-06"></div></td>
    </tr>
    <tr>
        <td><div class="gradient-07"></div></td>
        <td><div class="gradient-08"></div></td>
        <td><div class="gradient-09"></div></td>
    </tr>
    <tr>
        <td><div class="gradient-10"></div></td>
        <td><div class="gradient-11"></div></td>
        <td><div class="gradient-12"></div></td>
    </tr>
</table>
```

SASS:

```
div[class^="gradient-"]
  height: 200px
  width: 200px
  margin-bottom: 20px


//
.gradient-04
  background: red
  background: -webkit-radial-gradient(50% 50%, closest-side, red, black)
  background: -o-radial-gradient(50% 50%, closest-side, red, black)
  background: -moz-radial-gradient(50% 50%, closest-side, red, black)
  background: radial-gradient(closest-side at 50% 50%, red, black)

.gradient-05
  background: red
  background: -webkit-radial-gradient(10% 10%, closest-side, red, black)
  background: -o-radial-gradient(10% 10%, closest-side, red, black)
  background: -moz-radial-gradient(10% 10%, closest-side, red, black)
  background: radial-gradient(closest-side at 10% 10%, red, black)

.gradient-06
  background: red
  background: -webkit-radial-gradient(50% 10%, closest-side, red, black)
  background: -o-radial-gradient(50% 10%, closest-side, red, black)
  background: -moz-radial-gradient(50% 10%, closest-side, red, black)
  background: radial-gradient(closest-side at 50% 10%, red, black)

.gradient-07
  background: red
  background: -webkit-radial-gradient(50% 50%, closest-corner, red, black)
  background: -o-radial-gradient(50% 50%, closest-corner, red, black)
  background: -moz-radial-gradient(50% 50%, closest-corner, red, black)
  background: radial-gradient(closest-corner at 50% 50%, red, black)

.gradient-08
  background: red
  background: -webkit-radial-gradient(10% 10%, closest-corner, red, black)
  background: -o-radial-gradient(10% 10%, closest-corner, red, black)
```

```
    background: -moz-radial-gradient(10% 10%, closest-corner, red,
black)
    background: radial-gradient(closest-corner at 10% 10%, red, black)

.gradient-09
    background: red
    background: -webkit-radial-gradient(50% 10%, closest-corner, red,
black)
    background: -o-radial-gradient(50% 10%, closest-corner, red, black)
    background: -moz-radial-gradient(50% 10%, closest-corner, red,
black)
    background: radial-gradient(closest-corner at 50% 10%, red, black)

.gradient-10
    background: red
    background: -webkit-repeating-radial-gradient(50% 50%, closest-
corner,  red, black)
    background: -o-repeating-radial-gradient(50% 50%, closest-corner,
red, black)
    background: -moz-repeating-radial-gradient(50% 50%, closest-corner,
red, black)
    background: repeating-radial-gradient(closest-corner at 50% 50%,
red, black)

.gradient-11
    background: red
    background: -webkit-repeating-radial-gradient(10% 10%, closest-
corner, red, black)
    background: -o-repeating-radial-gradient(10% 10%, closest-corner,
red, black)
    background: -moz-repeating-radial-gradient(10% 10%, closest-corner,
red, black)
    background: repeating-radial-gradient(closest-corner at 10% 10%,
red, black)

.gradient-12
    background: red
    background: -webkit-repeating-radial-gradient(50% 10%, closest-
corner, red, black)
    background: -o-repeating-radial-gradient(50% 10%, closest-corner,
red, black)
    background: -moz-repeating-radial-gradient(50% 10%, closest-corner,
red, black)
    background: repeating-radial-gradient(closest-corner at 50% 10%,
red, black)
```

CSS:

```
div[class^="gradient-"] {
    height: 200px;
    width: 200px;
    margin-bottom: 20px;
}

.gradient-04 {
    background: red;
    background: -webkit-radial-gradient(50% 50%, closest-side, red,
black);
    background: -o-radial-gradient(50% 50%, closest-side, red, black);
    background: -moz-radial-gradient(50% 50%, closest-side, red,
black);
    background: radial-gradient(closest-side at 50% 50%, red, black);
}

.gradient-05 {
    background: red;
    background: -webkit-radial-gradient(10% 10%, closest-side, red,
black);
    background: -o-radial-gradient(10% 10%, closest-side, red, black);
    background: -moz-radial-gradient(10% 10%, closest-side, red,
black);
    background: radial-gradient(closest-side at 10% 10%, red, black);
}

.gradient-06 {
    background: red;
    background: -webkit-radial-gradient(50% 10%, closest-side, red,
black);
    background: -o-radial-gradient(50% 10%, closest-side, red, black);
    background: -moz-radial-gradient(50% 10%, closest-side, red,
black);
    background: radial-gradient(closest-side at 50% 10%, red, black);
}

.gradient-07 {
    background: red;
    background: -webkit-radial-gradient(50% 50%, closest-corner, red,
black);
    background: -o-radial-gradient(50% 50%, closest-corner, red,
black);
    background: -moz-radial-gradient(50% 50%, closest-corner, red,
black);
    background: radial-gradient(closest-corner at 50% 50%, red,
black);
}
```

```
.gradient-08 {
    background: red;
    background: -webkit-radial-gradient(10% 10%, closest-corner, red,
black);
    background: -o-radial-gradient(10% 10%, closest-corner, red,
black);
    background: -moz-radial-gradient(10% 10%, closest-corner, red,
black);
    background: radial-gradient(closest-corner at 10% 10%, red,
black);
}

.gradient-09 {
    background: red;
    background: -webkit-radial-gradient(50% 10%, closest-corner, red,
black);
    background: -o-radial-gradient(50% 10%, closest-corner, red,
black);
    background: -moz-radial-gradient(50% 10%, closest-corner, red,
black);
    background: radial-gradient(closest-corner at 50% 10%, red,
black);
}

.gradient-10 {
    background: red;
    background: -webkit-repeating-radial-gradient(50% 50%, closest-
corner, red, black);
    background: -o-repeating-radial-gradient(50% 50%, closest-corner,
red, black);
    background: -moz-repeating-radial-gradient(50% 50%, closest-
corner, red, black);
    background: repeating-radial-gradient(closest-corner at 50% 50%,
red, black);
}

.gradient-11 {
    background: red;
    background: -webkit-repeating-radial-gradient(10% 10%, closest-
corner, red, black);
    background: -o-repeating-radial-gradient(10% 10%, closest-corner,
red, black);
    background: -moz-repeating-radial-gradient(10% 10%, closest-
corner, red, black);
    background: repeating-radial-gradient(closest-corner at 10% 10%,
red, black);
}

.gradient-12 {
    background: red;
```

```
    background: -webkit-repeating-radial-gradient(50% 10%, closest-
corner, red, black);
    background: -o-repeating-radial-gradient(50% 10%, closest-corner,
red, black);
    background: -moz-repeating-radial-gradient(50% 10%, closest-
corner, red, black);
    background: repeating-radial-gradient(closest-corner at 50% 10%,
red, black);
}
```

Here's the effect in the browser:

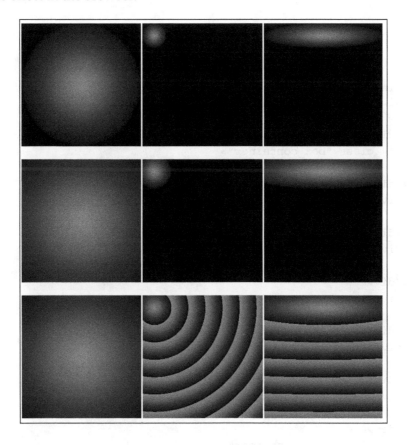

How to add box-shadow

Back in the day, shadow features weren't available in CSS. This feature gives you the opportunity to append the shadow effect to boxes (with `box-shadow`) and text (with `text-shadow`). How is `box-shadow` created? Let's check the parameters of this property in CSS:

```
box-shadow: horizontal-shadow vertical-shadow blur spread color
```

Before all parameters you can add inset. With this property shadow will be inside element.

The easiest way to understand this is to check how it behaves in the browser:

HTML:

```html
<div class="container">
    <div class="box_container">
        <div class="box__bottom_right">bottom right</div>
    </div>
    <div class="box_container">
        <div class="box__bottom_left">bottom left</div>
    </div>
    <div class="box_container">
        <div class="box__top_right">top right</div>
    </div>
    <div class="box_container">
        <div class="box__top_left">top left</div>
    </div>
    <div class="box_container">
        <div class="box__blurred">blurred</div>
    </div>
    <div class="box_container">
        <div class="box__notblurred">notblurred</div>
    </div>
    <div class="box_container">
        <div class="box__spreaded">spreaded</div>
    </div>
    <div class="box_container">
        <div class="box__innershadow">inner shadow</div>
    </div>
</div>
```

SASS:

```
=clearfix
  &:after
```

```
      content: ""
      display: table
      clear: both

  .container
    +clearfix
    width: 800px

    & > *
      float: left

  .box_container
    width: 200px
    height: 200px
    position: relative

  div[class^="box__"]
    width: 100px
    height: 100px
    position: absolute
    background: lightblue
    top: 50%
    left: 50%
    line-height: 100px
    font:
      size: 10px
    text:
      align: center
    transform: translate(-50%,-50%)

  .box__bottom_right
    box-shadow: 5px 5px 5px 0 #000

  .box__bottom_left
    box-shadow: -5px 5px 5px 0 #000

  .box__top_right
    box-shadow: 5px -5px 5px 0 #000

  .box__top_left
    box-shadow: -5px -5px 5px 0 #000

  .box__blurred
    box-shadow: 0px 0px 10px 0 #000

  .box__notblurred
    box-shadow: 0px 0px 0 0 #000

  .box__spreaded
    box-shadow: 0px 0px 0 5px #000

  .box__innershadow
    box-shadow: inset 0px 0px 5px 0px #000
```

CSS:

```css
.container {
    width: 800px;
}

.container:after {
    content: "";
    display: table;
    clear: both;
}

.container > * {
    float: left;
}

.box_container {
    width: 200px;
    height: 200px;
    position: relative;
}

div[class^="box__"] {
    width: 100px;
    height: 100px;
    position: absolute;
    background: lightblue;
    top: 50%;
    left: 50%;
    line-height: 100px;
    font-size: 10px;
    text-align: center;
    transform: translate(-50%, -50%);
}

.box__bottom_right {
    box-shadow: 5px 5px 5px 0 #000;
}

.box__bottom_left {
    box-shadow: -5px 5px 5px 0 #000;
}

.box__top_right {
```

```
        box-shadow: 5px -5px 5px 0 #000;
    }

.box__top_left {
        box-shadow: -5px -5px 5px 0 #000;
    }

.box__blurred {
        box-shadow: 0px 0px 10px 0 #000;
    }

.box__notblurred {
        box-shadow: 0px 0px 0 0 #000;
    }

.box__spreaded {
        box-shadow: 0px 0px 0 5px #000;
    }

.box__innershadow {
        box-shadow: inset 0px 0px 5px 0px #000;
    }
```

Here's the effect in the browser:

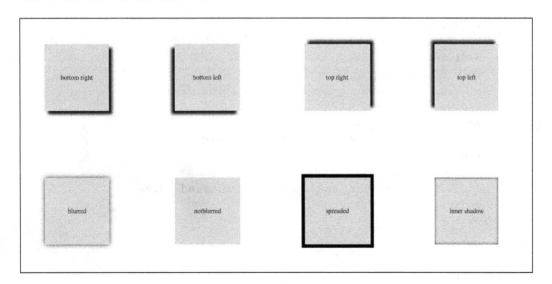

In this example, you can check how to set vertical and horizontal shadows. Additionally, you can set blur spread and its color. Adding a positive value to vertical and horizontal shadow moves the shadow to the bottom and right, respectively. When you are adding a negative value, it will move to the top and left.

How to add text-shadow

Adding a shadow for boxes is pretty simple. But how do we add a shadow to text? It is possible with the text-shadow property. It works in much the same way as box-shadow. Here's the definition:

```
text-shadow: horizontal-shadow vertical-shadow blur-radius color
```

Let's create an example based on the previous chapter's code to better understand the text-shadow property:

HTML:

```
<div class="container">
    <div class="box_container">
        <div class="box__bottom_right">bottom right</div>
    </div>
    <div class="box_container">
        <div class="box__bottom_left">bottom left</div>
    </div>
    <div class="box_container">
        <div class="box__top_right">top right</div>
    </div>
    <div class="box_container">
        <div class="box__top_left">top left</div>
    </div>
    <div class="box_container">
        <div class="box__blurred">blurred</div>
    </div>
    <div class="box_container">
        <div class="box__notblurred">notblurred</div>
    </div>
</div>
```

SASS:

```
=clearfix
  &:after
    content: ""
    display: table
```

```
    clear: both

.container
  +clearfix
  width: 00px

  &>*
    float: left

.box_container
  width: 100px
  height: 100px
  position: relative

div[class^="box__"]
  width: 100px
  height: 100px
  position: absolute
  background: lightblue
  top: 50%
  left: 50%
  line-height: 100px
  font:
    size: 10px
  text:
    align: center
  transform: translate(-50%,-50%)

.box__bottom_right
  text-shadow: 5px 5px 5px #000

.box__bottom_left
  text-shadow: -5px 5px 5px #000

.box__top_right
  text-shadow: 5px -5px 5px #000

.box__top_left
  text-shadow: -5px -5px 5px #000

.box__blurred
  text-shadow: 0px 0px 10px #000

.box__notblurred
  text-shadow: 5px 5px 0 red
```

CSS:

```
.container {
    width: 0px;
}

.container:after {
    content: "";
    display: table;
    clear: both;
}

.container >* {
    float: left;
}

.box_container {
    width: 100px;
    height: 100px;
    position: relative;
}

div[class^="box__"] {
    width: 100px;
    height: 100px;
    position: absolute;
    background: lightblue;
    top: 50%;
    left: 50%;
    line-height: 100px;
    font-size: 10px;
    text-align: center;
    transform: translate(-50%, -50%);
}

.box__bottom_right {
    text-shadow: 5px 5px 5px #000;
}

.box__bottom_left {
    text-shadow: -5px 5px 5px #000;
}

.box__top_right {
    text-shadow: 5px -5px 5px #000;
}

.box__top_left {
    text-shadow: -5px -5px 5px #000;
```

```
    }

    .box__blurred {
        text-shadow: 0px 0px 10px #000;
    }

    .box__notblurred {
        text-shadow: 5px 5px 0 red;
    }
```

Here's the effect in the browser:

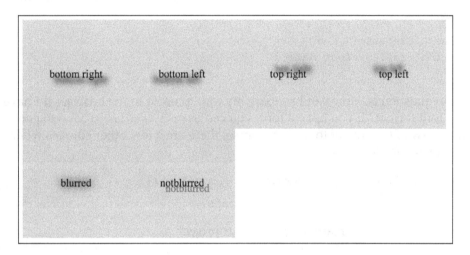

Additional font and text features

Font features in CSS have changed a lot in the past 5 years. Back in the day, there was no opportunity to use non-standard fonts and as it was described *safe for internet*. This was one of the issues that made Flash technology trendier, not only because of full Flash pages but because of **Scalable Inman Flash Replacement** (**SIFR**). With SIFR, you just needed to attach your font in Adobe Flash and compile the file; you could then use your font on the website. But you had a webpage in HTML with Flash instances. Then, there was a methodology based on JavaScript called **cufon**. You could use your font to visit the cufon page, compile your font, and then attach `cufon`. `js` on your website and your compiled font (JS file). In JavaScript, you needed to add which font should be swapped and finally your font was visible on the website.

Nowadays, we can use font-face and use custom fonts in the web version.

Using non-standard fonts in browsers

If you want to use your font in the browser, you need to prepare it. The basic definition of font-face is based on this example in raw CSS:

```
@font-face {
    font-family: font_name;
    src: url(your_font.woff);
}
```

If you want to use your font now, you will need to append this sample code in your CSS:

```
.classOfElement {
    font-family: font_name;
}
```

The main question is, How can I prepare my font to use it in the browser if I have another font format? If you have a font, you can use `fontsquirrel.com` to generate the final view of CSS ready to use. Of course, there are a few other sources where you can search for fonts:

- Google Fonts (`https://www.google.com/fonts`)
- Typekit (`https://typekit.com/fonts`)

Here, you can find fonts ready to use in your project.

Using CSS animations

CSS animations are a very useful feature. You don't need to use JavaScript for easy animations and CSS animations are supported by the GPU (short for Graphic Processing Unit). What can we do with CSS animations? Let's check the following example:

```
<div class="container">
    <div class="rollin"></div>
</div>
```

SASS:

```
.container
  width: 600px
  border: 1px solid #000

.rollin
  width: 100px
  height: 100px
```

```
    background: #000

    animation:
      duration: 1s
      name: roll_in
      iteration-count: 1
      delay: 1s
      fill-mode: backwards

  @keyframes roll_in
    from
      margin-left: 100%
      opacity: .3

    to
      margin-left: 0%
      opacity: 1
```

Here's the generated CSS:

```
.container {
    width: 600px;
    border: 1px solid #000;
}

.rollin {
    width: 100px;
    height: 100px;
    background: #000;
    animation-duration: 1s;
    animation-name: roll_in;
    animation-iteration-count: 1;
    animation-delay: 1s;
    animation-fill-mode: backwards;
}

@keyframes roll_in {
from {
        margin-left: 100%;
        opacity: 0.3;
    }
to {
        margin-left: 0%;
        opacity: 1;
    }
}
```

Here's the effect in the browser:

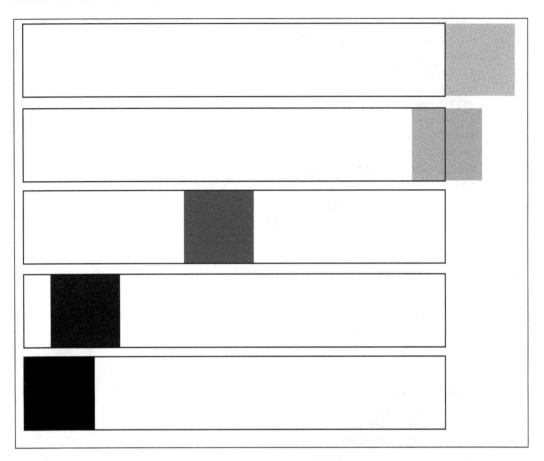

You can see the progress of animations, described in the SASS/CSS file.

The properties of CSS animations are:

- `animation-name`: This property defines which `@keyframs` definition should be used, for example: `animation-name: roll_in`
- `animation-delay`: This property defines the delay between the element loading and the animation starting, for example: `animation-delay: 2s`
- `animation-duration`: This property defines the length of the animation, for example: `animation-duration: 2s`
- `animation-iteration-count`: This property defines how many times the animation should be repeated, for example: `animation- iteration-count: 2`

- `animation-fill-mode`: This property defines how the element will behave with regard to the delay time, for example: `animation- fill-mode: backward`

How can I add an animation on hover? Let's create an example:

HTML:

```
<a href="" class="animation_hover">Element</a>
```

SASS:

```
.animation_hover
  display: inline-block
  padding: 20px
  background: #d3d3d3
  text-decoration: none
  color: black
  transition:
    duration: .5s
    property: all

  &:hover
    background: blue
    color: white
```

CSS:

```
.animation_hover {
    display: inline-block;
    padding: 20px;
    background: #d3d3d3;
    text-decoration: none;
    color: black;
    transition-duration: 0.5s;
    transition-property: all;
}

.animation_hover:hover {
    background: blue;
    color: white;
}
```

Here's the end result in the browser:

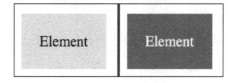

You can see the element before and after a hover action. Also, there is a transition that adds a little animation flavor to this button. What is important in this animation declaration?

```
transition-property
```

The preceding declaration gives a list of values that should be animated. An example of this list might be:

```
Color, background-color
```

This list means that the color and the background color will be animated. When you want to animate all properties, you can use *all* as a value.

Data attribute

Data attribute is mainly related to HTML code and JavaScript. With data attribute, you can describe DOM elements and use these values in scripts, for example, for sorting, animation, or any other purpose. But how can it help you in CSS code? Let's consider the following example.

Issue – bold on hover moves the navigation

This is a pretty common issue on websites. Let's imagine that you have inline elements that react to a hover. After hovering, the element changes its font-weight from normal to bold. The effect is that every element after the hovered element is shifted to the right. Let's begin with the HTML code:

```
<ul>
    <li><a href="#">First</a></li>
    <li><a href="#">Second</a></li>
    <li><a href="#">Third</a></li>
    <li><a href="#">Fourth</a></li>
    <li><a href="#">Fifth</a></li>
</ul>
```

SASS:

```
li, a
  display: inline-block
  text-align: center

a:hover
  font-weight: bold
```

CSS:

```
li, a {
    display: inline-block;
    text-align: center;
}

a:hover {
    font-weight: bold;
}
```

CSS:

```
li, a {
    display: inline-block;
    text-align: center;
}

a:hover {
    font-weight: bold;
}
```

The effect in the browser without and with hover action is:

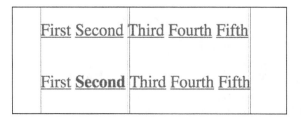

The red rulers are pointed shifts in structure. Now, let's use our *antidotum*. First, we need to slightly change our HTML code. This change is related to the `data-alt` attribute and its value. As a value, we are duplicating the value of the DOM element:

HTML:

```
<ul class="bold_list_fix">
    <li><a href="#" data-alt="First">First</a></li>
    <li><a href="#" data-alt="Second">Second</a></li>
    <li><a href="#" data-alt="Third">Third</a></li>
    <li><a href="#" data-alt="Fourth">Fourth</a></li>
    <li><a href="#" data-alt="Fifth">Fifth</a></li>
</ul>
```

SASS:

```
.bold_list_fix
  a::after
    display: block
    content: attr(data-alt)
    font-weight: bold
    height: 1px
    color: transparent
    overflow: hidden
    visibility: hidden
```

CSS:

```
.bold_list_fix a::after {
    display: block;
    content: attr(data-alt);
    font-weight: bold;
    height: 1px;
    color: transparent;
    overflow: hidden;
}
```

Voilà! Problem solved. As you can see, the trick is based on the `:after` pseudo element that is now kept as an invisible element. The content is set by taking an attribute from the HTML code with `attr(data-alt)`. To this content, the bold feature is added. This gives us enough space, which wasn't taken up in the previous code. Finally, the elements don't shift to the right.

Summary

In this chapter, we discussed CSS gradients so you don't need to make gradients with images. We analyzed the use of `box-shadow` and `text-shadow`. We created a simple animation and analyzed its parameters. Additionally, we used data-attribute in CSS code.

In the next chapter, we will discuss DRY (short for Don't Repeat Yourself) in CSS and try to create a basic framework that will be a starter for your projects.

10
Don't Repeat Yourself – Let's Create a Simple CSS Framework

How many times have you done some work, only to repeat it in the next project? How many times have you thought about elements that are repeatable? All the time when you are coding, you should think how many operations you can omit the next time you're working on the same or another project. This means that you need to use the following:

- Automatization
- Code templates or frameworks

This chapter is about building reusable code and how to finally use it as a foundation for projects. In this chapter, we will cover the following topics:

- Making a plan for a small and simple CSS framework
- Creating your own grid system
- Creating reusable elements

Remember that this code can and should be extended. Showed process should make you more aware about how you can help yourself with frameworks you've already created but that can still evolve with your code. Of course, you can use other frameworks.

File structure

File structure is very important when you are planning a system/framework. When you start creating something, it needs an evolution. So according to development process your system is evolving. It changes a lot when your system is evolving. So, let's create a simple structure:

- Useful mixins:
    - Short forms of useful elements
    - Inline list
    - Primitives
    - Clearfix
    - Simple gradient generators

- Grid mixins:
    - n of n grid

- Forms:
    - Input/textarea styling helpers
    - Input placeholders

- Buttons:
    - Inline (with auto-width)
    - Full-width

- Standard navigation:
    - One level
    - Two level

We will use mixins instead of already created classes. Why? We want to reduce CSS code as much as we can so that, when we generate full 12 grid, we will produce 12 classes in each breakpoint in media queries. As frontend developers, we want to create as much code as needed. Of course, we can reuse some classes and extend them with SASS, but the main approach of this framework is simple and reusable mixins.

Short forms of useful elements

In CSS code (and not only CSS), you wish to get the final effect more quickly each time you repeat a part of the code. So why don't you create short forms for some CSS declarations as well? Let's check what we can make shorter:

```
/* Text decoration */
=tdn
  text-decoration: none

=tdu
  text-decoration: underline


/* Text align */
=tac
  text-align: center

=tar
  text-align: right

=tal
  text-align: left


/* Text transform */
=ttu
  text-transform: uppercase

=ttl
  text-transform: lowercase


/* Display */
=di
  display: inline

=db
  display: block

=dib
  display: inline-block
```

```
/* Margin 0 auto */
=m0a
  margin: 0 auto
```

Now, each time you want to make some text uppercase, you are just using code:

```
.sampleClass
  +ttu
```

Here's the compiled CSS:

```
.sampleClass {
    text-transform: uppercase;
}
```

Another example of usage of short mixins is a element which will be displayed as a block element and text will be centered:

```
.sampleClass
  +db
  +tac
```

Here's the compiled CSS:

```
.sampleClass {
    display: block;
    text-align: center;
}
```

Other mixins

There are other mixins that are good for our framework:

- Gradients
- Animation
- Clearfix

Lets begin with gradient mixins:

```
=linearGradientFromTop($startColor, $endColor)
  background: $startColor /* Old browsers */
  background: -moz-linear-gradient(top,  $startColor 0%, $endColor
100%)
  background: -webkit-gradient(linear, left top, left bottom, color-
stop(0%, $startColor), color-stop(100%, $endColor))
  background: -webkit-linear-gradient(top,  $startColor 0%, $endColor
100%)
  background: -o-linear-gradient(top,  $startColor 0%, $endColor 100%)
```

```
  background: -ms-linear-gradient(top,  $startColor 0%, $endColor
100%)
  background: linear-gradient(to bottom,  $startColor 0%, $endColor
100%)
  filter: progid:DXImageTransform.Microsoft.gradient(
startColorstr='#{$startColor}', endColorstr='#{$endColor}',GradientTy
pe=0 )

=linearGradientFromLeft($startColor, $endColor)
  background-color: $startColor
  background: -webkit-gradient(linear, left top, right top,
from($startColor), to($endColor))
  background: -webkit-linear-gradient(left, $startColor, $endColor)
  background: -moz-linear-gradient(left, $startColor, $endColor)
  background: -ms-linear-gradient(left, $startColor, $endColor)
  background: -o-linear-gradient(left, $startColor, $endColor)
  background: linear-gradient(left, $startColor, $endColor)
  filter: progid:DXImageTransform.Microsoft.gradient(startColorStr='#{
$startColor}', endColorStr='#{$endColor}', gradientType='1')
```

Animate all:

```
=animateAll($time)
  -webkit-transition: all $time ease-in-out
  -moz-transition: all $time ease-in-out
  -o-transition: all $time ease-in-out
  transition: all $time ease-in-out
```

Clearfix

Don't forget to add `clearfix` to your mixins in your private SASS framework. You will be using it as an invocation of a mixin or as a class, and all the other elements will extend the previously created class:

```
=clearfix
  &:after
    content: " "
    visibility: hidden
    display: block
    height: 0
    clear: both
```

Each time you wish to create a reusable `clearfix` class, you can do it this way:

```
.clearfix
  +clearfix
```

Here's the compiled CSS:

```
.clearfix:after {
    content: " ";
    visibility: hidden;
    display: block;
    height: 0;
    clear: both;
}
```

Or a shorter version can be written as:

```
.cf
  +clearfix
```

Here's the compiled CSS:

```
.cf:after {
    content: " ";
    visibility: hidden;
    display: block;
    height: 0;
    clear: both;
}
```

Now, you can extend it with @extend in SASS code:

```
.element
  @extend .cf
```

Here's the compiled CSS:

```
.cf:after, .element:after {
    content: " ";
    visibility: hidden;
    display: block;
    height: 0;
    clear: both;
}
```

Center an absolute element in an other relative element:

```
/* Absolute center vertically and horizontally */
=centerVH
  position: absolute
  top: 50%
```

```
left: 50%
-ms-transform: translate(-50%,-50%)
-webkit-transform: translate(-50%,-50%)
transform: translate(-50%,-50%)
```

Media queries

In each responsive web project, you will need to create media queries. You need to choose steps that you will implement and then start creating the project based on these steps.

Media queries template

Media queries are rather simple to use and create. The main problem with media queries is reusable steps that you can keep in one place. In some projects, you will need to add a few more queries because of project visibility problems or some extra code that will affect your code. Let's focus on how to make it once with some settings and then use it in our code.

The basic settings are focused on the following:

- Mobile devices (phones)
- Mobile devices (tablets)
- Desktop devices
- Desktop devices (large)

In some cases, you can extend this list with mobile device position (portrait and landscape), but a smaller number of media queries is better and easier for maintenance. So how can we keep the sizes?

- `$small`: 320px
- `$medium`: 768px
- `$large`: 1024px

Grids

In standard HTML/CSS projects the most repeatable element is grid. Of course, you can use somebody else's grid or take it from a CSS framework such as Bootstrap or Foundation. Is it hard to create it from scratch? Not really. In this chapter, we will create a basic grid system and will use it to see how it creates rows and columns.

Standard grids 16/12

The standard grid is based on a 16-column or 12-column system. What are the advantages of both systems? It depends on your structure. For example, after analyzing the layout, say you need:

- 3-column composition
- 2-column composition
- 6-column composition

So, you can use the 12-columns system. However, as you can see, you need to stick to this system, so how can you create your own code so it's more elastic? You can use the following naming convention:

```
.grid-NofK
```

Here, N is the number of columns and K is the divider, for example:

```
.grid-3of12
.grid-5of6
```

When you are working with grids, you need to remember that sometimes you need to push some columns from the left. This is the case when you need to create .push classes:

```
.push-NofK
```

What are the pros of this naming convention? There is no static divider. In classic grids, you have a grid with 12 columns or 16 columns and their combinations. Here's a sample of grids written class by class:

Grid of 12:

```
.grid-1of12 {
    width: 8.33%
}

.push-1of12 {
    margin-left: 8.33%
}

.grid-2of12 {
    width: 16.66%
}

.push-2of12 {
```

```
        margin-left: 16.66%
    }

    .grid-3of12 {
        width: 25%
    }

    .push-3of12 {
        margin-left: 25%
    }

    .grid-4of12 {
        width: 33.33%
    }

    .push-4of12 {
        margin-left: 33.33%
    }

    .grid-5of12 {
        width: 41.66%
    }

    .push-5of12 {
        margin-left: 41.66%
    }

    .grid-6of12 {
        width: 50%
    }

    .push-6of12 {
        margin-left: 50%
    }

    .grid-7of12 {
        width: 58.33%
    }

    .push-7of12 {
        margin-left: 58.33%
    }

    .grid-8of12 {
```

```
        width: 66.66%
    }

    .push-8of12 {
        margin-left: 66.66%
    }

    .grid-9of12 {
        width: 75%
    }

    .push-9of12 {
        margin-left: 75%
    }

    .grid-10of12 {
        width: 83.33%
    }

    .push-10of12 {
        margin-left: 83.33%
    }

    .grid-11of12 {
        width: 91.66%
    }

    .push-11of12 {
        margin-left: 91.66%
    }

    .grid-12of12 {
        width: 100%
    }

    .push-12of12 {
        margin-left: 100%
    }
```

Grid of 16:

```
    .grid-1of16 {
        width: 6.25%
    }
```

```css
.push-1of16 {
    margin-left: 6.25%
}

.grid-2of16 {
    width: 12.5%
}

.push-2of16 {
    margin-left: 12.5%
}

.grid-3of16 {
    width: 18.75%
}

.push-3of16 {
    margin-left: 18.75%
}

.grid-4of16 {
    width: 25%
}

.push-4of16 {
    margin-left: 25%
}

.grid-5of16 {
    width: 31.25%
}

.push-5of16 {
    margin-left: 31.25%
}

.grid-6of16 {
    width: 37.5%
}

.push-6of16 {
    margin-left: 37.5%
}
```

```css
.grid-7of16 {
    width: 43.75%
}

.push-7of16 {
    margin-left: 43.75%
}

.grid-8of16 {
    width: 50%
}

.push-8of16 {
    margin-left: 50%
}

.grid-9of16 {
    width: 56.25%
}

.push-9of16 {
    margin-left: 56.25%
}

.grid-10of16 {
    width: 62.5%
}

.push-10of16 {
    margin-left: 62.5%
}

.grid-11of16 {
    width: 68.75%
}

.push-11of16 {
    margin-left: 68.75%
}

.grid-12of16 {
    width: 75%
}
```

```
.push-12of16 {
    margin-left: 75%
}

.grid-12of16 {
    width: 81.25%
}

.push-12of16 {
    margin-left: 81.25%
}

.grid-12of16 {
    width: 87.5%
}

.push-12of16 {
    margin-left: 87.5%
}

.grid-12of16 {
    width: 93.75%
}

.push-12of16 {
    margin-left: 93.75%
}

.grid-12of16 {
    width: 100%
}

.push-12of16 {
    margin-left: 100%
}
```

That was a lot of writing...

Now, we need to create a code that we can use in media queries and on responsive websites. In the most popular CSS frameworks such as Bootstrap and Foundation, you can use classes for phones/tablets/desktops:

```
<div class="small-2 medium-4 large-5">
</div>
```

For example, when the divider is set to 12, you will see this box on small devices with 2 columns wide, on medium devices 4 columns wide, and on large documents 5 columns wide. We can create all of these classes, but I recommend you create a mixin that we can invoke in each element described in CSS.

The SASS Code will look like this:

```
=grid($columns, $divider)
  width: percentage($columns/$divider)

=push($columns, $divider)
  margin-left: percentage($columns/$divider)
```

How can we use it in SASS code? Let's imagine that we have a block based on grid 16 and we want to give it width of 12 of 16 and push it with 2 of 16:

```
.gridElement
  +grid(12, 16)
  +push(2, 16)
```

Here's the compiled CSS:

```
.gridElement {
    width: 75%;
    margin-left: 12.5%;
}
```

Standard reusable structures

As a frontend developer, you are always struggling with repeatable elements. In almost all cases, you feel as if you are trying to reinvent the wheel, so what can you do to not repeat yourself? Let's create a few standard and reusable structures.

Reusable multilevel menus

A multilevel menu is the most reusable code. All bigger websites have a menu that you can describe as reusable code.

Let's begin with the HTML code:

```html
<ul class="menu-multilevel">
    <li>
        <a href="#">Level one - item one</a>
        <ul>
            <li><a href="#">Level two - item one</a></li>
```

```html
            <li><a href="#">Level two - item two</a></li>
            <li><a href="#">Level two - item three</a></li>
            <li><a href="#">Level two - item four</a></li>
        </ul>
    </li>
    <li>
        <a href="#">Level two - item one</a>
        <ul>
            <li><a href="#">Level two - item one</a></li>
            <li><a href="#">Level two - item two</a></li>
            <li><a href="#">Level two - item three</a></li>
            <li><a href="#">Level two - item four</a></li>
        </ul>
    </li>
    <li>
        <a href="#">Level one - item three</a>
        <ul>
            <li><a href="#">Level three - item one</a></li>
            <li><a href="#">Level three - item two</a></li>
            <li><a href="#">Level three - item three</a></li>
            <li><a href="#">Level three - item four</a></li>
        </ul>
    </li>
</ul>
```

SASS code:

```scss
ul.menu-multilevel
  list-style: none
  padding: 0

ul.menu-multilevel > li
  float: left
  display: inline-block
  position: relative
  margin-right: 10px

  &:hover
    ul
      display: block
      width: 200px

ul.menu-multilevel ul
  display: none
```

```
    position: absolute
    left: 0

  li
    display: block
```

Here's the compiled CSS:

```
ul.menu-multilevel {
    list-style: none;
    padding: 0;
}

ul.menu-multilevel > li {
    float: left;
    display: inline-block;
    position: relative;
    margin-right: 10px;
}

ul.menu-multilevel > li:hover ul {
    display: block;
    width: 200px;
}

ul.menu-multilevel ul {
    display: none;
    position: absolute;
    left: 0;
}

ul.menu-multilevel ul li {
    display: block;
}
```

Now, let's rebuild this code a little to create a reusable mixin in SASS:

```
=memuMultilevel
  list-style: none
  padding: 0

  & > li
    float: left
    display: inline-block
    position: relative
```

```
      margin-right: 10px

      &:hover
        ul
          display: block
          width: 200px

    & ul
      display: none
      position: absolute
      left: 0

      li
        display: block
```

To use it, you will need to invoke a mixin like this:

```
ul.menu-multilevel
  +memuMultilevel
```

The generated CSS:

```
ul.menu-multilevel {
    list-style: none;
    padding: 0;
}

ul.menu-multilevel > li {
    float: left;
    display: inline-block;
    position: relative;
    margin-right: 10px;
}

ul.menu-multilevel > li:hover ul {
    display: block;
    width: 200px;
}

ul.menu-multilevel ul {
    display: none;
    position: absolute;
    left: 0;
}
```

```
ul.menu-multilevel ul li {
    display: block;
}
```

How to create reusable buttons

Buttons are the next elements that you can see and reuse. Let's think about button parameters. For sure, we need to have the opportunity to set the background and font color. We need to have an opportunity to change the border color and padding.

Let's begin with a simple CSS definition:

```
.button {
    padding: 5px 10px;
    background: #ff0000;
    color: #fff;
}
```

So based on this, the mixin can look as follows in SASS:

```
=button($bgc, $fc)
  display: inline-block
  background: $bgc
  color: $fc
```

Here:

- $bgc: Background color
- $fc: Font color

To use this mixin, you just need to execute this:

```
.button
  padding: 5px 10px
  +button(#ff0000, #fff)
```

Here's the compiled CSS:

```
.button {
    padding: 5px 10px;
    display: inline-block;
    background: #ff0000;
    color: #fff;
}
```

How can you extend this mixin? Let's think about other values that you can parameterize. For sure, a border radius. So, let's add a new mixin:

```
=roundedButton($bgc, $fc, $bc, $br)
  background: $bgc
  color: $fc
  border-color: $bc
  border-radius: $br
```

Here:

- `$bc`: border color
- `$br`: border radius

Let's use this mixin:

```
.roundedButton
  +roundedButton(black, white, red, 5px)
```

Here's the compiled CSS:

```
.roundedButton {
    background: black;
    color: white;
    border-color: red;
    border-radius: 5px;
}
```

If you need to create a bunch of buttons with three sizes, you can do it like this:

```
.button
  +button(#ff0000, #fff)

  .small
    padding: 5px 10px

  .medium
    padding: 10px 20px

  .large
    padding: 15px 30px
```

Here's the compiled CSS:

```
.button {
    display: inline-block;
    background: #ff0000;
```

```
    color: #fff;
}

.button .small {
    padding: 5px 10px;
}

.button .medium {
    padding: 10px 20px;
}

.button .large {
    padding: 15px 30px;
}
```

Gathering other reusable mixins

What we need is a bunch of useful and reusable mixins. What can be additionally helpful? Let's think:

- Primitives
- Inline lists

Primitives

As you can remember from one of the previous chapters, we have been using primitives. List of mixins which creates primitives can be very useful and helpful part of our framework. We will we have mixins for:

- Rectangle (with and without a fill)
- Circle/ring
- Triangle

Let's have a quick reminder:

```
=rectangle($w, $h, $c)
  width: $w
  height: $h
  background: $c

=square($w, $c)
  width: $w
  height: $w
```

```
    background: $c

=circle($size, $color)
  width: $size
  height: $size
  border-radius: 50%
  background: $color

=ring($size, $color, $width)
  width: $size
  height: $size
  border-radius: 50%
  border: $width solid $color
  background: none

=triangleRight($width, $height, $color)
  width: 0
  height: 0
  border-style: solid
  border-width: $height/2 0 $height/2 $width
  border-color: transparent transparent transparent $color

=triangleLeft($width, $height, $color)
  width: 0
  height: 0
  border-style: solid
  border-width: $height/2 $width $height/2 0
  border-color: transparent $color transparent transparent

=triangleTop($width, $height, $color)
  width: 0
  height: 0
  border-style: solid
  border-width: 0 $width/2 $height $width/2
  border-color: transparent transparent $color transparent

=triangleBottom($width, $height, $color)
  width: 0
  height: 0
  border-style: solid
  border-width: $height $width/2 0 $width/2
  border-color: $color transparent transparent transparent
```

Let's test and use our framework

To check how our framework is working and how easy it is to append all of our stuff, let's create a blog template. In this template, let's include views:

- List of posts
- Single post
- Single page

Let's create regions:

- Header
- Footer
- Content

Here's our simplified design:

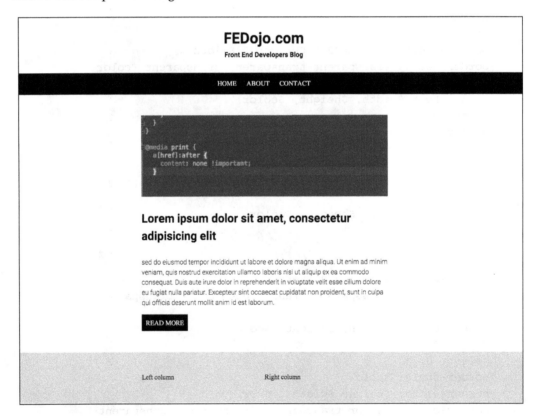

Let's begin with the simple structure of a blog page (the Home page):

```html
<!DOCTYPE html>
<html>
<head>
    <meta charset="utf-8">
    <title></title>
    <link rel="stylesheet" href="css/master.css" media="screen"
title="no title" charset="utf-8">
</head>
<body>
<header>
    <h1>FEDojo.com</h1>
    <h2>Front End Developers Blog</h2>
</header>

<nav>
    <ul>
        <li><a href="#">Home</a></li>
        <li><a href="#">About</a></li>
        <li><a href="#">Contact</a></li>
    </ul>
</nav>

<main>
    <article class="main--article">
        <a href="#">
            <img src="img/error_log.png" alt=""/>
            <span class="comments"></span>
        </a>
        <h3>Lorem ipsum dolor sit amet, consectetur adipisicing elit</
h3>
        <p>
            sed do eiusmod tempor incididunt ut labore et dolore magna
aliqua. Ut enim ad minim veniam, quis nostrud
            exercitation ullamco laboris nisi ut aliquip ex ea commodo
consequat. Duis aute irure dolor in reprehenderit
            in voluptate velit esse cillum dolore eu fugiat nulla
pariatur. Excepteur sint occaecat cupidatat non
            proident, sunt in culpa qui officia deserunt mollit anim
id est laborum.
        </p>
        <a href="#" class="readmore">Read more</a>
    </article>

</main>

<footer>
    <div class="wrapper">
        <div class="column">
```

```
                Left column
            </div>
            <div class="column">
                Right column
            </div>
        </div>
    </footer>
</body>
</html>
```

As you can see, we have a structure based on tags:

- Header
- Nav
- Main
- Footer

This is our file structure:

Let's describe the header:

```
header
  h1
    +tac
    margin-bottom: 0

  h2
    +tac
    font-size: 16px
    margin-top: 0
    margin-bottom: 30px
```

Describing the footer:

```
footer
  width: 100%
  background: #d3d3d3
  padding: 50px 0

  .wrapper
    +m0a /* margin 0 auto */
    +clearfix
    max-width: $wrapper

  .column
    width: 50%
    float: left
```

Describing the navigation:

```
nav
  background: black
  text-align: center

  ul
    +navigation

  a
    color: white
    +ttu
    padding: 10px
```

In the `fed` directory, we store our reusable code (our framework). In the remaining directories, we store code related to the project. In describing the structure, we store styles of elements that repeat on all views. In the views directory, we will keep styles for elements related to specific views.

Remember!

When you are creating some reusable code or even any other code, you need to leave comments. For some reason, there is a current (and discourteous) trend for programmers not to add comments "their code doesn't need additional description." Another school of thought is, "That's my code. I understand what I am writing". Do you think it is fair to leave it as it is? Of course, the answer is no! Even your memory isn't perfect. You can forget what you mean in your code and what the purpose was. It is recommended you at least write short comments for yourself and other people who will work on the project.

In the golden era of Github and Bitbucket, you can share your code in seconds and work with another programmer from another part of the world who can fork your code or contribute to your project.

Summary

As you can see, there are a lot of reusable structures that you can decorate each time you create a new project. It's better to write something once and then add some new functionalities, rather than write something every time and describe repeatable elements.

In the next chapter, we will try to create a simple CSS framework with components ready to use!

11
Mailers Fundamentals

This chapter is about building mailers and the fundamental aspects of creating the right structure. Because building the right structure for a mailer is not easy and it is still related to the old school thinking about HTML structure, there are only a handful of tutorials that show how to do it from beginning to end. Why? Let's begin!

In this chapter, we will cover:

- Creating a simple structure for a mailer
- Finding out what is and isn't possible in mailers
- Comparing the most known mailer clients, including Outlook and Gmail
- Getting back to the old school thinking of HTML structure based on tables

Testing your mailer

The process of testing e-mail is complicated because of the bunch of e-mail clients which you need to install on your computer. This is of course related to operating systems which you will need to install the following:

- Microsoft Outlook 2007/2010/2013
- Microsoft Outlook 2003/Express
- Microsoft Outlook.com
- iPhone Mail
- Apple Mail
- Gmail
- Yahoo! e-mail

This bunch of e-mail clients is rather long and it is going to be problematic to test all of them. But you can use in your workflow some email testers. There is a list of online tools which you can use for example Litmus which will be described later in this chapter.

Back to tables

Tables structure is the most popular methodology of building bulletproof e-mail templates. It looks like a blast from the past. So, let's bring the flavor of the past and let's start creating the right structure:

```
<!DOCTYPE html PUBLIC "-//W3C//DTD XHTML 1.0 Transitional//EN"
"http://www.w3.org/TR/xhtml1/DTD/xhtml1-transitional.dtd">
<html xmlns="http://www.w3.org/1999/xhtml">
<head>
    <meta http-equiv="Content-Type" content="text/html;
charset=utf-8"/>
    <meta name="viewport" content="width=device-width"/>
    <meta name="format-detection" content="telephone=no">
    <title>Untitled Document</title>
</head>
<body>
<style type="text/css">
    .class {} /* here will be your code */
</style>
<table width="100%" border="0" cellspacing="0" cellpadding="0">
    <!-- HERE your content -->
</table>
</body>
</html>
```

You might ask, "But where is the HTML5 declaration and why aren't styles included with the link `rel` tag?" It is because of the old HTML interpreters included in e-mail clients and the use of a newer `doctype` can create problems with compatibility. For now, we have a skeleton. Let's begin writing the styles:

So why are we using this part of the code?

```
<meta name="format-detection" content="telephone=no">
```

This code is related to an iOS-specific problem. It changes the behavior of an input telephone number, which (on iOS) is detected and changed to an interactive link that you can click and start a phone call.

Resetting styles

In CSS code, there is a lot of code that should be used to reset a behavior over all browsers. The same situation occurs in mailers. There is a bunch of declarations that you should append to your style section and that will help you to provide a bulletproof mailer. So what can we add as a resetter?

```
body {
    margin: 0;
    padding: 0;
    min-width: 100% !important;
}
```

The first declaration with removal of the margin and padding is very important. This declaration is known from standard Internet browsers. As you can see, the `min-width` occurs too. As described in the code, this is very important line to check! In the value, there is `100% !important`. Yes! There is no space between the value and `!important`. The following code is a part of `reset` styles for emailers:

```
body,
table,
td,
a {
    -webkit-text-size-adjust: 100%; // IOS specific
-ms-text-size-adjust: 100%; // Windows mobile
}


.ExternalClass {
    width: 100%;
}

.ExternalClass,
.ExternalClass p,
.ExternalClass span,
.ExternalClass font,
.ExternalClass td,
.ExternalClass div {
    line-height: 100%;
}
```

What is `ExternalClass`? This class is related to templates that will be displayed in Outlook or Hotmail. It's a good approach to set this bunch of classes into your `<style>` tag. This will minimize the problems that can occur on specific e-mail clients. The following code contains mso- prefixes. This means that it is related to Microsoft Office.

```
table {
    mso-table-lspace: 0pt;
    mso-table-rspace: 0pt;
}
```

This code is related to Microsoft Outlook. It will reset the additional space in the border:

```
#outlook a{
    padding:0;
}


h1,
h2,
h3,
h4,
h5,
h6 {
    color: <your_color>!important;
}

h1 a,
h2 a,
h3 a,
h4 a,
h5 a,
h6 a {
    color: <your_color>!important;
}

h1 a:active,
h2 a:active,
h3 a:active,
h4 a:active,
h5 a:active,
h6 a:active {
    color: <your_color>!important;
}

h1 a:visited,
```

```
h2 a:visited,
h3 a:visited,
h4 a:visited,
h5 a:visited,
h6 a:visited {
    color: <your_color>!important;
}

img{
    -ms-interpolation-mode:bicubic;
    border: 0;
    height: auto;
    line-height: 100%;
    outline: none;
    text-decoration: none;
}
```

Targeting specific devices through media queries

To build a bulletproof mailer, you will need to use specific code for some specific e-mail clients and devices. This is more difficult to do because of the problems with debugging (there is no good debugger/inspector to check behaviors live). Which devices do we need? Let's create a list:

- iPad or iPhone with retina and non-retina display
- Android devices with:
    - Low density (pixel ratio smaller than 1)
    - Medium density (pixel ratio equal to 1)
    - High density (pixel ratio greater than 1)

```
@media only screen and (max-device-width: 480px) {
}
```

This set with which you will match tablets and small screens:

```
@media only screen and (min-device-width: 768px) and (max-device-width: 1024px) {
}
```

Retina display is known from iOS devices such as iPhones, iPods, and iPads. These devices can be targeted with this media query:

```
@media only screen and (-webkit-min-device-pixel-ratio: 2) {
}
```

Target low density Android layouts:

```
@media only screen and (-webkit-device-pixel-ratio: .75) {
}
```

Target medium density Android layouts:

```
@media only screen and (-webkit-device-pixel-ratio: 1) {
}
```

Target high density Android layouts:

```
@media only screen and (-webkit-device-pixel-ratio: 1.5) {
}
```

If you want to target Outlook 2007 and 2010, you will need to use an HTML conditional construction. This will look like this:

```
<!--[if gte mso 9]>
<style>
    /* Your code here */
</style>
<![endif]-->
```

CSS properties in e-mail templates

It is important to remember which properties you can use and what the exceptions are. This knowledge will keep you from a lot of nervous situations. Let's list them:

Property	Problems for specific client/device
direction	-
font	-
font-family	-
font-style	-
font-variant	-
font-size	-
font-weight	-
letter-spacing	-

Property	Problems for specific client/device
`line-height`	(iOS) Default size of font is 13px
`text-align`	(Outlook) Don't append line-height to TD element. It is recommended to append this property to P element.
`text-decoration`	-
`text-indent`	-
`background`	(Outlook) No support for background images
`background-color`	-
`border`	-
`padding`	(Outlook) Padding is not supported for elements: `<p>` `<div>` `<a>`
`width`	(Outlook) Width is not supported for elements: `<p>` `<div>` `<a>`
`list-style-type`	-
`border-collapse`	-
`table-layout`	-

As you can see, there are a lot of properties that don't work the same way on all e-mail clients. This is a big problem, but with a basic knowledge you will be aware which element can be described in CSS. The biggest problem in mailers is positioning, which is not supported. So for example in most cases when the text overflows some image you will need to use image which includes your text.

Responsive e-mail templates

This part of the book can start a big discussion because the building of responsive e-mails is not possible at all in all e-mail clients. This is a working draft that can be used as a base for your e-mailers:

```
<!DOCTYPE html PUBLIC "-//W3C//DTD XHTML 1.0 Transitional//EN"
        "http://www.w3.org/TR/xhtml1/DTD/xhtml1-transitional.dtd">
<html xmlns="http://www.w3.org/1999/xhtml">
<head>
    <title>Our responsive template</title>
```

```
    <meta charset="utf-8">
    <meta name="viewport" content="width=device-width, initial-
scale=1">
    <meta http-equiv="X-UA-Compatible" content="IE=edge"/>
    <style type="text/css">
        @media screen and (max-width: 525px) {
            .wrapper {
                width: 100% !important;
            }

            .content {
                padding: 10px 5% 10px 5% !important;
                text-align: left;
            }
        }
    }
</style>
</head>
<body style="margin: 0 !important;
padding: 0 !important;">


<table border="0"
        cellpadding="0"
        cellspacing="0"
        width="100%">
    <tr>
        <td bgcolor="#ffffff"
            align="center"
            style="padding: 10px;">
            <table border="0"
                    cellpadding="0"
                    cellspacing="0"
                    width="500"
                    class="wrapper">
                <tr>
                    <td>
                        <table width="100%"
                                border="0"
                                cellspacing="0"
                                cellpadding="0">
                            <tr>
                                <td align="left"
                                    style="font-size: 40px;
font-family: Helvetica, Arial, sans-serif;
color: #000000;
                                    padding-top: 10px;"
```

```
                                class="content">Header of our mailer
                            </td>
                        </tr>
                        <tr>
                            <td align="left"
                                style="padding: 20px 0 0 0;
            font-size: 16px;
            line-height: 25px;
            font-family: Helvetica, Arial, sans-serif;
            color: #000000;
            padding-bottom: 30px;"
class="content">Lorem ipsum dolor sit amet, consectetur adipiscing
elit. Sed
                                varius, leo a ullamcorper feugiat,
ante purus sodales justo, a faucibus libero lacus
                                a est. Aenean at mollis ipsum.
                            </td>
                        </tr>
                        <tr>
                            <td align="center" class="content">
                                <table width="100%"
                                    border="0"
                                    cellspacing="0"
                                    cellpadding="0">
                                    <tr>
                                        <td align="left">
                                            <table
                                                    border="0"
                                                    cellspacing="0"
                                                    cellpadding="0">
                                                <tr>
                                                    <td
                                                    align="center"
                                                    bgcolor="#000">
                                                    <a href="#"
                                                    target="_blank"
                                                    style="font-size: 20px;
                font-family: Helvetica, Arial, sans-serif;
                color: #ffffff;
                text-decoration: none;
                color: #ffffff;
                text-decoration: none;
                padding: 10px 20px;
    display: inline-block;">
                                                        Lorem ipsum click
                                                    </a>
                                                    </td>
                                                </tr>
```

```
                                                    </table>
                                                 </td>
                                              </tr>
                                           </table>
                                        </td>
                                     </tr>
                                  </table>
                               </td>
                            </tr>
                         </table>

                   </td>
                </tr>

            </table>

         </body>
         </html>
```

As you can see, there is a lot of code… but the effect is not so great when we want to compare it to the normal website. The following screenshot shows how it will look in a desktop browser with width greater than 520px:

Header of our mailer

Lorem ipsum dolor sit amet, consectetur adipiscing elit. Sed varius, leo a ullamcorper feugiat, ante purus sodales justo, a faucibus libero lacus a est. Aenean at mollis ipsum.

Lorem ipsum click

In smaller browsers (smaller than 520 px), you will see this:

Header of our mailer

Lorem ipsum dolor sit amet, consectetur adipiscing elit. Sed varius, leo a ullamcorper feugiat, ante purus sodales justo, a faucibus libero lacus a est. Aenean at mollis ipsum.

Lorem ipsum click

Inlining the e-mail template

The inlining of an e-mail template is a very important process before pushing your project when you are using a separate CSS file or the CSS code is written in the `<style>` section—`http://foundation.zurb.com/e-mails/inliner-v2.html`.

Tips for e-mail template development

Like the other processes related to frontend development, this should start with the prepared designs. Real web designers know where the borders are for a good website and should know where the borders related to the e-mailers are located. There are a lot of restrictions in global e-mailers' creation process. That's why the designer involved in this process should know the features that can be used in HTML e-mail templates.

The e-mail template framework INK by ZURB

This development process is simpler, with some framework that gathers tested fragments of code. ZURB, after creating the great Front End framework called Foundation, created INK as a framework for e-mail templates. For full information about this framework, it is recommended that you visit `http://foundation.zurb.com/e-mails.html`.

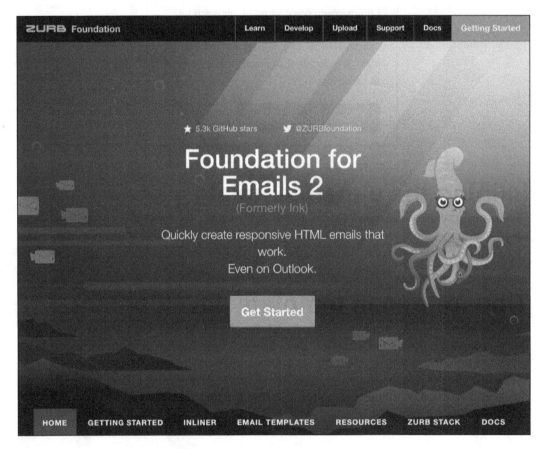

Creation of Email template based on INK is very developer friendly. Framework gathered a lot of easy to use components like grid system, buttons, thumbnails which you can easily add to your template. Additionally there is a list of adjustable parameters like gutter, global paddings and margins. For deeper understanding of ZURB INK2 framework it is recommended to check official documentation: `http://foundation.zurb.com/emails/docs/`.

Testing with Litmus

Testing of email templates is pretty complicated when you want to gather all of testing environments. Its going to be easier when you will use Litmus which makes a screenshots of your email template in most known email clients.

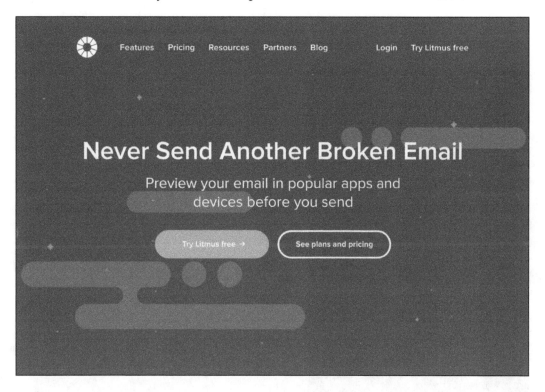

After creating of your template you will need to copy your HTML code and paste it into the system. If your e-mail has some images hosted on some server you can send an email to your account in Litmus. Litmus creates on application side your dedicated email address. When you send email to this address you can test this email in Litmus.

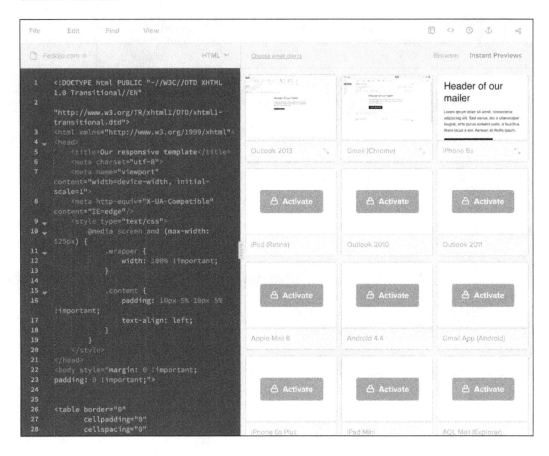

As you can see on screen above you can check your code in most known email clients. Screenshot was made on trial version of Litmus account that why some of views are not activated.

Summary

Preparing bulletproof e-mail templates is a complicated process. Why? As you can see, HTML and CSS behave pretty strangely and are not logical when you are familiar with standard web browsers. Of course, all of these processes can be described and there is a workflow that will help you to build the mailer without nervous situations. The list of restrictions brought by e-mail templates is very long, but good knowledge of the basics and experience in e-mail template development can make you a specialist in this frontend niche.

In the next chapter, we will discuss the scalability and modularity of CSS code. You will get to know more about methodologies and naming conventions. Let's start!

12
Scalability and Modularity

In this chapter, we'll cover the most well-known CSS methodologies in the process of creating modular and scalable code. This is a very interesting subject because there are a lot of methodologies. Each has its pros and cons. In this chapter, we will get a basic knowledge about them.

We will cover the following topics:

- Building scalable and modular code
- CSS methodologies
- SMACSS
- BEM
- OOCSS
- How to choose the right methodology?

Building scalable and modular code

The process of building good code is unique to each developer. But how can you build easily scalable CSS code? Additionally, this code needs to be modular.

The most important thing in methodologies is the naming convention. You can use a proper methodology for your project, but you can use it in the wrong way and append bad class names. Have you ever seen projects that have classes with a name and definition similar to this one:

```
.padding-0 {
    padding: 10px;
}
```

As you can see, the class name is created to make padding with value 0, but finally it has a value not equal to 0. This can be an example of a bad naming convention. There can be more examples of badly used names:

```
.marginTop10 {
    padding-top: 50px;
}
```

The second important thing in methodologies is the structure of classes/elements in document and nesting levels. Some sources say that the maximum nesting levels shouldn't be greater than five, while others say three. For the sake of readability, code should have a fully flat structure (with one level).

Let's check the popular CSS methodologies and learn their best features.

CSS methodologies

CSS methodologies are built to make the process of building code more predictable and more organized. The most well-known methodologies are as follows:

- **Scalable and Modular Architecture for CSS (SMACSS)**
- **Object Oriented CSS (OOCSS)**
- **Block Element Modifier (BEM)**

Each of these methodologies has different features. Let's check what these popular methodologies can offer.

SMACSS

SMACSS was created by Jonathan Snook. It's more of a framework than a methodology:

For the official website of the project, visit `https://smacss.com/`.

SMACSS is based on the following rules:

- Base rules
- Layout rules
- Module rules
- State rules
- Theme rules

Base rules

Base rules are related elements:

- header (`h1-h6`)
- links (`a`, `a:hover`, `a:active`)
- forms (`form`, `input`)

All of these rules are related to HTML elements and should not require the `!important` statement.

Layout rules

Layout rules are related to the main blocks in the structure, such as these:

- `header`
- `footer`
- `content`
- `side menu`
- `article`

These elements are described with IDs as follows:

CSS:

```
#header {
    display: inline-block;
}

#footer {
    display: inline-block;
    padding: 10px;
}
```

Module rules

Module rules are related to components or blocks on the website. Let's take an example fragment of a previously created structure for a blog post. Here, we will have a better overview of how to use the SMACSS modules in this specific case:

To describe it in CSS, we will need to use selectors based on the following:

```
.module > element / class
```

Let's build an HTML for it:

```
<article class="article">
    <img src="#">
    <h1>Lorem ipsum dolor sit amet, consecteur adisiciping elit</h1>
    <p> Lorem ipsum … </p>
    <a href="#">Read more</a>
</article>
```

Let's create selectors based on module rules:

```
.article >img {
    /* Image in top */
}

.article > h1 {
    /* Post header */
}

.article > p {
    /* Post excerpt */
}

.article > a {
    /* Read more button */
}
```

It's pretty easy and obvious how to create all of this.

State rules

State rules are related to elements' states. There are a bunch of possible state rules classes. Here's a list of possible rules:

- `is-collapsed`
- `is-error`
- `is-active`
- `is-tab-active`

The easiest way to describe state rules is an example with a simple navigation:

```
<nav>
    <ul>
        <li class="is-active"><a href="#">Home</a>
            <ul>
                <li><a href="#">Home 1.1</a></li>
                <li><a href="#">Home 1.2</a></li>
            </ul>
        </li>
        <li><a href="#">About</a></li>
        <li><a href="#">Contact</a></li>
        <ul>
</nav>
```

To describe an element in a menu which is currently active, you can use the class `is-active`. This convention is easy to read and gives you the opportunity for the right class names.

Theme rules

Theme rules are related to specific views. For example, you created a page with an element:

The HTML is as follows:

```
<body>
    <div class="alert">
        Alert
    </div>
</body>
```

All we know in the beginning is that `.alert` is a window and needs to stick to the browser like a lightbox window.

The CSS (in `alert.css`) is as follows:

```css
.alert {
    width: 300px;
    height: 300px;
    position: fixed;
    left: 50%;
    top: 50%;
    transform: translate(-50%, -50%);
}
```

Now we need to add a specific theme for this `.alert` (in `theme.css`):

```css
.alert {
    background: red;
    color: black;
}
```

As we can see in `alert.css`, we keep the definition of static elements that won't be changed in `theme.css`. Theme rules kept in `theme.css` are theming our component; in this case, it is an `alert` window.

Summary of SMACSS

SMACSS is a really good methodology due to the following reasons:

* It has base rules that gather definitions of main elements
* It has state rules that describe the states of elements with the `is-` convention
* It uses IDs for main elements in CSS

OOCSS

OOCSS is a project or methodology started by Nicole Sullivan:

Object-Oriented CSS

Hosted

Play with these in Firebug to learn the basics.

Template
Grids
Module
Content (very alpha)

Downloads on Github

Velocity download
Alternate download

Stuck?

If you don't keep up with any of the exercises you can view (and download) the finished examples here.

Starting Template
Exercise 1: Template
Exercise 2: Grids
Exercise 3: Module Manipulation
Exercise 4 Module Creation

Stubbornella, Github, FAQ

Welcome, Velocity Conference participants!

All the resources you need to get started are linked from the left navigation. Start by downloading the base files. Exercises one and two can be completed in Firebug if you are comfortable with it. Then you can download the finished file at the beginning of Exercise 3.

Visit the official website of the project at `http://oocss.org/` for more information.

The main principles of OOCSS are as follows:

- Separate structure and skin
- Separate container and content

What does it mean? Let's try to dig a little bit deeper.

This means that it is better to describe an element that is nested in another element with a separate class than nested in a container. When you create a code like this:

```
<div class="product">
    <h1>Name of product</h1>
    <p>Description</p>
</div>
```

You shouldn't base your CSS on selectors:

```
.product h1 {}
.product p {}
```

But rather on small change in markup:

```
<div class="product">
    <h1 class="product-name">Name of product</h1>
    <p class="product-desc">Description</p>
</div>
```

And then describe it in CSS with selectors:

```
.product-name {}
.product-desc {}
```

It gives you the possibility to move the class .product-name to any element in the HTML structure and the visual features will be changed too, as described. This gives you more flexibility and reusable code.

Using OOCSS in our sample

Let's try to use OOCSS in our sample code to describe the blog post:

```
<article class="article">
    <img src="#" class="article-image">
    <h1 class="article-h1">Lorem ipsum dolor sit amet, consecteur
adisiciping elit</h1>
    <p class="article-p"> Lorem ipsum … </p>
    <a href="#" class="article-btn">Read more</a>
</article>
```

In your CSS, it will look like this:

```
.article { /**/}
.article-image { /**/ }
.article-h1 { /**/ }
.article-p { /**/ }
.article-btn { /**/ }
```

Summary of OOCSS

Let's summarize OOCSS:

- You can reuse classes anywhere in your HTML and you don't need to think about which module it was described in
- The methodology is very mature

Block Element Modifier (BEM)

The next methodology is built by Yandex. In the BEM methodology, every element is described with a class. Nesting isn't needed because of the flat CSS structure. The naming convention is based on:

Visit the official website of the project at `https://en.bem.info/` for more information.

Using BEM in our sample

Let's try to use BEM in our sample code to describe the blog post:

```
<article class="article">
    <img src="#" class="article__image">
    <h1 class="article__h1">Lorem ipsum dolor sit amet, consecteur
adisiciping elit</h1>
    <p class="article__p"> Lorem ipsum … </p>
    <a href="#" class="article__btn">Read more</a>
</article>
```

Now in your CSS, it will look like this:

```
.article { /**/}
.article__image { /**/ }
.article__h1 { /**/ }
.article__p { /**/ }
.article__btn { /**/ }
```

Using BEM in SASS

It shouldn't be hard to build BEM code in SASS. Let's try to describe the code from the previous code:

```
.article
  &__image
    /* Image in top */

  &__h1
    /* Post header */

  &__p
    /* Post paragraph */

  &__btn
    /* Post button */
```

How to use modifier?

The preceding code example is based on blocks and elements from the BEM methodology. How can we add M with its modifier? When can we use it? Let's imagine that we have two articles: one article with an image on the left and a second with an image on the right-hand side of the block. With the BEM methodology, we can use a modifier. Let's take the previous CSS code and append the modifier:

```
.article { /**/}
.article__image { /**/ }
.article__h1 { /**/ }
.article__p { /**/ }
.article__btn { /**/ }

.article--imgleft { /**/}
.article--imgleft__image { /**/ }
.article--imgleft__h1 { /**/ }
.article--imgleft__p { /**/ }
.article--imgleft__btn { /**/ }
```

As we can see, the modifier is defined as `imgleft` and is added to the block using two dashes. The modifier can help you to avoid creating new code for the new block. It can work like a decorator implemented in CSS.

Which methodology should you use?

This is a very good question. For sure, you need to use the methodology that works for you. But which one is suitable? The best CSS methodology is the one that can be easily debugged. When is it? For sure, when you don't need to dig, for example, 10 rules for one element. The best readability in CSS can be achieved when the rule is strictly related to the elements on the page.

Maybe your own methodology?

Yes! If you want to create something new and best for your project, create your own methodology. However, do not reinvent the wheel and do not try to rename the well-known methodologies to build your own. A deep understanding of these three methodologies can be the key for you to create a small, unnamed mash-up that fits your requirements.

Summary

Choosing the proper methodology for your code/project should be easier now. In this chapter, we acquainted ourselves with CSS methodologies and tried to define their approaches. The most important thing is to understand them and know how to apply them to your code. It can be useful in the process of debugging some other code.

In the next chapter, we will focus on CSS code optimization. We will use `Gulp.js` to prepare your code for testing and final optimized projects.

13
Code Optimization

This chapter is about building code and the processes that are related to every step of creating the code in general. There are a few general stages of this process and we will study how we can optimize code at each of these steps.

In this chapter, we will cover the following topics:

- Code optimization at each step of creation
- How to keep code in your repository
- How to optimize SASS code
- How to use short forms in CSS/SASS code
- How to prepare code for production

Self-optimization

The optimization process starts when you start writing code. Awareness of what you can optimize and how it should appear during writing a code is essential. After the writing process, when you start optimization, it can be pretty hard to refactor and restructure the code. But it is easy to build code and automatically append optimization processes. Which of these processes can you perform during the writing of code?

- Usage of short forms
- Omit usage of `!important`
- Omit usage of IDs

A few steps before you push code live

In the code creation process, there are a few repeatable steps:

- Writing code
- Testing code
- Pushing code live

The processes are sometimes repeatable, especially when they are related to projects built in *The Lean Startup* methodology by Eric Ries and projects with multiple stages. You need to remember these few steps before you push code live:

- Check whether short forms are used
- Check whether elements/declarations are duplicated
- Check whether elements/declarations are used in HTML (zombie selectors)
- Check the appearance of `!important` (if possible, try to omit them)
- Check whether the code is minified

This list is pretty basic. In the next sections, we will run through the optimization processes and usage, for checking all the possibilities.

Using short forms

Short forms are very helpful to minify code during writing and after the building process. Using short forms in CSS, you can save a lot of characters and make the code slimmer. Let's look at an overview of short forms.

Short forms of paddings/margins

How many times have you been writing paddings and margins with full forms? How many times does it happen that you are reading somebody's code and seeing that they are not using short forms for margins and paddings makes you nervous? Yes! It can make you nervous because it is a waste of CSS! Let's start with simple description of an element's padding in SASS:

```
.element
  padding:
    top: 10px
    right: 20px
    bottom: 30px
    left: 40px
```

It will give you CSS code like this:

```
.element {
    padding-top: 10px;
    padding-right: 20px;
    padding-bottom: 30px;
    padding-left: 40px;
}
```

Here's a short way to describe it in CSS:

```
.element
  padding: 10px 20px 30px 40px
```

In general, padding can be described as follows:

```
padding: top right bottom left
```

You can do the same thing with margins:

```
.element
margin:
    top: 10px
    right: 20px
    bottom: 30px
    left: 40px
```

It will give you CSS code like this:

```
.element {
    margin-top: 10px;
    margin-right: 20px;
    margin-bottom: 30px;
    margin-left: 40px;
}
```

Here's a short way to describe it in CSS:

```
.element
margin: 10px 20px 30px 40px
```

In general, the margin can be described as follows:

```
margin: top right bottom left
```

Let's use another example:

```
.element
  margin:
    top: 10px
    right: 20px
    bottom: 10px
    left: 20px
```

Compiled to CSS:

```
.element {
  margin-top: 10px;
  margin-right: 20px;
  margin-bottom: 10px;
  margin-left: 20px;
}
```

As you can see, there are two pairs of values. When the value of the top margin/padding is repeated in the bottom value and the left value is equal to the right value, you can use the short version:

```
.element
  margin: 10px 20px
```

When compiled to CSS, it looks like this:

```
.element {
  margin: 10px 20px;
}
```

As you can see, the version is minified and finally based on the pattern:

```
margin: top_bottom_value left_right_value
```

Short forms of borders

Let's start with the basic description of a border, and then we can extend it:

```
.element
  border:
  style: solid
  color: #000
  width: 10px
```

Here's the compiled CSS:

```
.element {
  border-style: solid;
  border-color: #000;
  border-width: 10px;
}
```

This class will create a border around the box, which will be solid with 10px width and its color will be black. So, let's create a class that will include all the borders (top, right, bottom, and left) with a defined style color and width:

```
.element
  border:
    top:
       style: solid
       color: #000
       width: 1px

    right:
       style: solid
       color: #f00
       width: 2px

    bottom:
       style: solid
       color: #0f0
       width: 3px

    left:
       style: solid
       color: #00f
       width: 4px
```

CSS:

```
.element {
  border-top-style: solid;
  border-top-color: #000;
  border-top-width: 1px;

  border-right-style: solid;
  border-right-color: #f00;
  border-right-width: 2px;
```

```
        border-bottom-style: solid;
        border-bottom-color: #0f0;
        border-bottom-width: 3px;

        border-left-style: solid;
        border-left-color: #00f;
        border-left-width: 4px;
    }
```

So if you want to make this a little bit shorter, you can use a mix of global definitions of shorten border. The code is as follows:

```
.element
  border: 1px solid #000
```

CSS:

```
.element {
  border: 1px solid #000;
}
```

And directions. The code will look like this:

```
.element
border:
    top: 1px dotted #000
    right: 2px solid #f00
    bottom: 3px dashed #0f0
    left: 4px double #00f
```

Compiled:

```
.element {
    border-top: 1px dotted #000;
    border-right: 2px solid #f00;
    border-bottom: 3px dashed #0f0;
    border-left: 4px double #00f;
}
```

There is a way to describe style/width/color in the same way we define padding and border:

```
.element
  border:
    style: dotted solid dashed double
    width: 1px 2px 3px 4px
    color: #000 #f00 #0f0 #00f
```

Compiled:

```
.element {
    border-style: dotted solid dashed double;
    border-width: 1px 2px 3px 4px;
    border-color: #000 #f00 #0f0 #00f;
}
```

Now, let's gather information about `border-radius`. The global definition of border radius is as follows:

SASS:

```
.element
  border-radius: 5px
```

CSS:

```
.element {
    border-radius: 5px;
}
```

Describe each corner in another line and another value:

```
.element
  border:
    top:
      left-radius: 5px
      right-radius: 6px
    bottom:
      left-radius: 7px
      right-radius: 8px
```

CSS:

```
.element {
  border-top-left-radius: 5px;
  border-top-right-radius: 6px;
  border-bottom-left-radius: 7px;
  border-bottom-right-radius: 8px;
}
```

Now, the preceding code can be described this way to make it shorter:

```
.element
  border-radius: 5px 6px 7px 8px
```

CSS:

```
.element {
  border-radius: 5px 6px 7px 8px;
}
```

Short forms in fonts styling

Fonts are described in every paragraph header link. As you can see, it's good to use shorthand for so many repeated occurrences in the code. Here, we have a simple description of the font and line height of a sample element:

```
.element
font:
    size: 12px
    family: Arial
    weight: bold
  line-height: 1.5
```

CSS:

```
.element {
  font-size: 12px;
  font-family: Arial;
  font-weight: bold;
  line-height: 1.5;
}
```

Let's use a short form based on pattern:

```
font: font_family font_size/line_height font_weight
```

With this short form, our five lines in SASS (four lines in CSS) are changed to one line:

```
.element
  font: Arial 12px/1.5 bold
```

After compilation, the code is as follows:

```
.element {
  font: Arial 12px/1.5 bold;
}
```

Short forms in backgrounds

Background is one of the most commonly used CSS features. The main use of background is:

```
.element
  background:
    color: #000
    image: url(path_to_image.extension)
    repeat: no-repeat
    attachment: fixed
    position: top left
```

This code will give us the following output:

```
.element {
    background-image: url(path_to_image.extension);
    background-repeat: no-repeat;
    background-attachment: fixed;
    background-position: top left;
}
```

It's a lot of code! The short form is described in this order:

```
background-color
background-image
background-repeat
background-attachment
background-position
```

Example:

```
background: url color repeating attachment position-x position-y;
```

If we want to describe our element with this short form, we just need to make it this way:

```
.element
  background: #000 url(path_to_image.extension) no-repeat fixed top
left
```

After SASS compilation in CSS, we will get the following:

```
.element {
  background: #000 url(path_to_image.extension) no-repeat fixed top
left;
}
```

Checking repetitions

When you are creating the code in CSS, you need to be aware of the repetitions of your code. The code can look a little bit weird for professional developers, but we can treat it as a great sample of the code review process. Let's analyze it.

HTML:

```
<section>
    <a class="button">click it</a>
    <a class="buttonBlue">click it</a>
    <a class="buttonGreen">click it</a>
</section>
```

CSS:

```
section .button {
    padding: 5px 10px; /* Repeated padding */
    font-size: 12px; /* Repeated font size */
    color: white; /* Repeated color */
    background: black;
}

section .buttonBlue {
    padding: 5px 10px; /* Repeated padding */
    font-size: 12px; /* Repeated font size */
    color: white; /* Repeated color */
    background: blue;
}

section .buttonGreen {
    padding: 5px 10px; /* Repeated padding */
    font-size: 12px; /* Repeated font size */
    color: white; /* Repeated color */
    background: green;
}
```

As you can see, the repetitions are commented and we will create a general class now:

```
section .button {
    padding: 5px 10px;
    font-size: 12px;
    color: white;
    background: black;
```

```
}

section button.button_blue {
    background: blue;
}

section button.button_green {
    background: green;
}
```

We will need to append small changes in the HTML code:

```
<section>
    <a class="button">click it</a>
    <a class="button button_blue">click it</a>
    <a class="button button_green">click it</a>
</section>
```

To minify it in SASS:

```
section
  .button
    padding: 5px 10px
    font-size: 12px
    color: white
    background: black

    &.button_blue
      background: blue

    &.button_green
      background: green
```

Here's another method to deal with repetitions without changing the markup:

```
article .h1 {
    font-family: Arial; /* Repeated font family */
    padding: 10px 0 15px 0; /* Repeated padding */
    font-size: 36px;
    line-height: 1.5; /* Repeated line height */
    color: black; /* Repeated color */
}

article .h2 {
    font-family: Arial; /* Repeated font family */
    padding: 10px 0 15px 0; /* Repeated padding */
```

```
    font-size: 30px;
    line-height: 1.5; /* Repeated line height */
    color: black; /* Repeated color */
}

article .h3 {
    font-family: Tahoma; /* Oryginal font family */
    padding: 10px 0 15px 0; /* Repeated padding */
    font-size: 24px;
    line-height: 1.5; /* Repeated line height */
    color: black; /* Repeated color */
}
```

Let's gather the repetitions:

```
font-family: Arial;
padding: 10px 0 15px 0;
line-height: 1.5;
color: black;
```

Let's add a value that will be overwritten in custom element .h3:

```
font-family: Tahoma;
```

Now, let's describe the selectors and overwrite the values in separate selectors:

```
article .h1,
article .h2,
article .h3 {
    padding: 10px 0 15px 0;
    line-height: 1.5;
    color: black;
    font-family: Arial;
}

article .h1 {
    font-size: 36px;
}

article .h2 {
    font-size: 30px;
}

article .h3 {
    font-size: 24px;
    font-family: Tahoma;
}
```

Let's change it to SASS code:

```
article
.h1,
  .h2,
  .h3
    padding: 10px 0 15px 0
    line-height: 1.5
      color: black
    font:
      family: Arial

  .h1
    font:
      size: 36px

  .h2
    font:
      size: 30px

  .h3
    font:
      size: 24px
      family: Tahoma
```

Let's do the same with `@extend`:

```
article
  .h1
    padding: 10px 0 15px 0
    line-height: 1.5
    color: black
    font:
      family: Arial
      size: 36px

  .h2
    @extend .h1
    font:
      size: 30px

  .h3
    @extend .h1
    font:
      size: 24px
      family: Tahoma
```

The process of checking the repetitions is easy when you are creating the code yourself, but it can be harder when you are working with other developers or when you are working on a project which was started by somebody else. This process makes the code shorter, so it can be treated as a process of code optimization. With these techniques, you can append changes to your code.

Summary

In this chapter, we discussed the process of CSS code optimization. With this knowledge, you can minify your code and you can think about optimization processes during the creation of code. This knowledge will make you a more aware frontend developer who knows how code can be minified in a jiffy.

In the next chapter, we will discuss the final automatizations that you can use in CSS and frontend projects!

14
Final Automatization and Processes Optimization

In this last chapter, we will discuss a final automatization of repeatable processes during the creation of CSS code. There are a lot of processes that can be automatized, but awareness of whether it can be done and knowledge of the tools to be used is essential. In this chapter, we will focus on tools and how to implement automatizations in the Gulp task runner.

In this chapter, we will cover the following topics:

- Images on retina and mobile devices
- How to recognize unused CSS
- How to minify the code
- How to make a screenshots from the list of pages for quicker overview
- How to use the basics of Jade templating and append its compilation into Gulp

Gulp

At the beginning of this book, I introduced Gulp as a starter for SASS. But using Gulp just to compile SASS can be a waste of time. In this chapter, we will add more tasks to Gulp, which can be used as a frontend developer and which will help you to optimize your code.

Jade as your templating engine

Writing HTML files can be problematic in the case of bigger projects. The maintenance of repeatable elements of a page, such as main navigation footer sidebars, can be a problem when you need to work with, for example, 10 files. Each time you want to change something in the footer, you will need to update 10 files. The situation becomes more complicated when a project has 50 templates. You can start using, for example, PHP or any language that includes files with repeatable parts of code or use one of the template languages. There are multiple templating systems. Some of the well-known and trendy ones are listed here:

- Handlebars
- HAML
- Jade
- Slim

Let's focus on Jade. Why? Because of the following features:

- Mixins support
- Master templates
- Partialization of files
- Indented syntax (similar to SASS)

Installing and using Jade

Jade is installed by node package manager. You can install it with the following command:

```
npm install jade --global
```

If you want to compile some file, you just need to invoke the HTML file as follows:

```
jade filename.html
```

For more information, I recommend you to check the official documentation of the Jade templating system at http://jade-lang.com/.

Basics of Jade

It is good to have a theoretical introduction, but let's try to describe this part of the code into Jade:

```
<nav>
    <ul>
        <li><a href="#">Home</a></li>
        <li><a href="#">About</a></li>
        <li><a href="#">Contact</a></li>
    </ul>
</nav>
```

In Jade, it will look like this:

```
nav
    ul
        li
            a(href="#") Home
        li
            a(href="#") About
        li
            a(href="#") Contact
```

You can see that you don't need to think about the standard HTML problem "is my tag closed?" Indentations are keeping track of the opening and closing of tags. Each text that you want to append into a tag appears after a space after the tag description (name and attributes). Let's take a look at this part of the code:

```
a(href="#") Home
```

This part of code will be compiled to:

```
<a href="#">Home</a>
```

As you can see, in Jade, an attribute (href) appeared after element name (a), which is described in brackets. Let's take the next part of the HTML code that we will translate to Jade:

```
<head>
    <meta charset="utf-8">
    <title>Page title</title>
    <link rel="stylesheet" href="css/main.css" media="screen"
title="no title" charset="utf-8">
</head>
```

This part of the code will be repeating on all pages because it contains the `head` tag of our HTML. In Jade, it will look like this:

```
head
    meta(charset="utf-8")
    title Page title
    link(rel="stylesheet", href="css/main.css", media="screen",
title="no title", charset="utf-8")
```

Here you can see how to append more attributes to the HTML element. In the `link` element, each attribute in brackets is separated with commas.

The next part of the code is related to the DOM elements with classes and IDs:

```
<main id="main">
    <article class="main--article">
        <a href="#">
            <img src="img/error_log.png" alt=""/>
            <span class="comments"></span>
        </a>
        <h3>Lorem ipsum dolor sit amet, consectetur adipisicing elit</
h3>
        <p>
            sed do eiusmod tempor incididunt ut labore et dolore
        </p>
        <a href="#" class="readmore">Read more</a>
    </article>
</main>
```

In Jade, the code looks like this:

```
main#main
    article.main--article
        a(href="#")
            img(src="img/error_log.png", alt="Error log")
            .comments
        h3 Lorem ipsum dolor sit amet
        p sed do eiusmod tempor incididunt ut labore et dolore
        a(href="#").readmore Read more
```

You can see that you don't need to describe this part:

```
<main id="main">
```

This is written as:

```
main(id="main")
```

There is a short form in Jade:

```
main#main
```

The same situation with classes:

```
<article class="main--article">
```

You can use a short form too:

```
article.main--article
```

This short method makes Jade easy to understand because it is based on selectors used in CSS.

Mixins in Jade

Mixins in Jade are very useful, especially when you have some repeatable elements on the web page. This can be, for example, some small element like a with `href`:

```
mixin link(href, name)
    a(href= href)=name
```

All we need to do now to invoke it is just add it in your template:

```
+link("url", "Your link")
```

And in your compiled file, you will see:

```
<a href="url">Your link</a>
```

Include and extend functions in Jade

As mentioned before, we can keep parts of code in separate files. The easiest way to do it is the `include` method. Let's imagine that we have defined the main nav in the file `navigation.jade` and we want to append its content in our template. The code is as follows:

File name is: `navigation.jade`

```
nav
    ul
        li
            a(href="#") Home
        li
            a(href="#") About
        li
            a(href="#") Contact
```

File name is: `template.jade`

```
doctype html
html
    head
        meta(charset="utf-8")
        title Page title
        link(rel="stylesheet", href="css/main.css", media="screen",
title="no title", charset="utf-8")

    body
        include _navigation.jade
```

When you compile `template.jade`, you will get:

```
<!DOCTYPE html>
<html>
<head>
    <meta charset="utf-8">
    <title>Page title</title>
    <link rel="stylesheet" href="css/main.css" media="screen" title="no
title" charset="utf-8">
</head>
<body>
<nav>
    <ul>
        <li><a href="#">Home</a></li>
        <li><a href="#">About</a></li>
        <li><a href="#">Contact</a></li>
    </ul>
</nav>
</body>
</html>
```

This is a great moment to use a master layout that can be extended. This can be done with code manipulation. The first manipulation has to be made in the master template — define a block that will be swapped in our HTML file. The second needs to be done in the file that will represent a final HTML file — point master template which will be extended. The code is as follows:

File name is: `master.jade`

```
doctype html
html
    head
        meta(charset="utf-8")
```

```
    title Page title
        link(rel="stylesheet", href="css/main.css", media="screen",
title="no title", charset="utf-8")

    body
        include _navigation.jade
        block content
```

File name is: `index.jade`

```
extends master

block content
    h1 Content
```

Compiled document:

```
<!DOCTYPE html>
<html>
<head>
    <meta charset="utf-8">
    <title>Page title</title>
    <link rel="stylesheet" href="css/main.css" media="screen" title="no
title" charset="utf-8">
</head>
<body>
<nav>
    <ul>
        <li><a href="#">Home</a></li>
        <li><a href="#">About</a></li>
        <li><a href="#">Contact</a></li>
    </ul>
</nav>
<h1>Content</h1>
</body>
</html>
```

Jade in gulp.js

To create or add Jade tasks in `gulpfile.js`, you need to install a specific package with npm: `gulp-jade`. To do so, use the following command:

```
npm install --save gulp-jade
```

Then you need to define a new task in `gulpfile.js` and add a watcher for templates, which will be stored in the `src/jade` directory. Here's a listing of the extended `gulpfile.js` from the first chapter of this book:

```
var gulp = require('gulp'),
    sass = require('gulp-sass'),
    jade = require('gulp-jade');

gulp.task('sass', function () {
    return gulp.src('src/css/main.sass')
        .pipe(sass().on('error', sass.logError))
        .pipe(gulp.dest('dist/css/main.css'));
});

gulp.task('jade', function() {
    gulp.src('src/jade/*.jade')
        .pipe(jade())
        .pipe(gulp.dest('dist/'));
});

gulp.task('default', function () {
    gulp.watch('src/sass/*.sass', ['sass']);
    gulp.watch('src/jade/*.jade', ['jade']);
});
```

How will it behave? Every time you change any of the files in the folder `src/jade`, compiled files will land in the `dist` folder. Of course, this structure can be changed if you wish; this is just sample of usage. Feel free to change it!

UnCSS

How many times have you faced a situation where some classes/selectors are not used in HTML but are described in CSS code? This happens every time your project is changed or redesigned. For example, your task is to remove some section and add a few more lines in the HTML code. So you will add some CSS code and then remove some of it. But are you sure that the CSS code doesn't contain unused CSS portions of code? UnCSS will help you to finish this task. To install it, you need to execute this command:

```
npm install -g uncss
```

Let's take a look at the flags used in the npm command:

Flag	Description
-g	Global installation
--save	Local installation
	These packages will appear in package.json in the section dependencies.
	These packages are needed to run your app in production.
--save-dev	Local installation
	These packages will appear in package.json in the section devDependencies.
	These packages are needed for development and testing processes.

Integrating UnCSS in Gulp

First, we need to install gulp-uncss through npm:

```
npm install --save gulp-uncss
```

Now, we need to add new tasks in gulpfile.js. We will need to create a test stage in our project, which will be stored in the test directory. You need these new tasks to make a process based on uncss:

```
gulp.task('clean-css-test', function () {
    return gulp.src('test/css/main.css', {read: false})
        .pipe(rimraf({force: true}));
});

gulp.task('jade-test', function() {
    return gulp.src('src/jade/templates/*.jade')
        .pipe(jade())
        .on('error', gutil.log)
        .pipe(gulp.dest('test/'));
});

gulp.task('sass-test',['clean-css-test'], function () {
    return gulp.src('src/sass/main.sass')
        .pipe(sass().on('error', sass.logError))
        .pipe(gulp.dest('test/css/'));
});
```

```
gulp.task('uncss',['jade-test', 'sass-test'], function () {
    return gulp.src('test/css/main.css')
        .pipe(uncss({
            html: ['test/**/*.html']
        }))
        .pipe(gulp.dest('./test/uncss'));
});
```

To run the uncss task, you need to use the following command:

```
gulp uncss
```

This command will perform the following tasks:

- Compile Jade files to the test folder
- Remove old CSS files from the test folder
- Compile SASS files to the test folder
- Run the uncss task and save the document with only the used part of CSS in the test/uncss folder

Now we need to test it live. We will prepare a short testing environment.

Here's the structure of the files:

```
├── jade
│   ├── master_templates
│   │   └── main.jade
│   ├── partials
│   │   ├── footer.jade
│   │   └── navigation.jade
│   └── templates
│       ├── about.jade
│       ├── contact.jade
│       └── index.jade
└── sass
    └── main.sass
```

The code is as follows:

File name is: main.jade

```
doctype html
html
    head
        meta(charset="utf-8")
        title Page title
```

```
        link(rel="stylesheet", href="css/main.css", media="screen",
title="no title", charset="utf-8")

    body
        include ../partials/navigation
        block content
        include ../partials/footer
```

File name is: navigation.jade

```
nav
    ul
        li
            a(href="#") Home
        li
            a(href="#") About
        li
            a(href="#") Contact
```

File name is: footer.jade

```
footer
    p Copyright fedojo.com
```

File name is: index.jade

```
extends ../master_templates/main

block content
    .main
        p Test of INDEX page
```

File name is: about.jade

```
extends ../master_templates/main

block content
    .main
        h1 Test of ABOUT page
```

File name is: contact.jade

```
extends ../master_templates/main

block content
    .main
        h1 Test of CONTACT page
```

File name is: `main.sass`

```
body
background: #fff

p
color: #000

.header
background: #000
color: #fff

.footer
background: #000
color: #fff

header
background: #000
color: #fff

footer
background: #000
color: #fff
```

Now, let's check whether the process was good for us. This is the file compiled from SASS:

```
body {
  background: #fff;
}

p {
  color: #000;
}

.header {
  background: #000;
  color: #fff;
  }

.footer {
  background: #000;
  color: #fff;
  }
```

```
header {
 background: #000;
 color: #fff;
}

footer {
 background: #000;
 color: #fff;
}
```

This file is checked by `uncss`, which looked into all the templates (`index.html`, `about.html`, and `contact.html`):

```
body {
 background: #fff;
}

p {
 color: #000;
}

footer {
 background: #000;
 color: #fff;
}
```

Our new command built with Gulp removed all unnecessary CSS declarations.

Minifying CSS

Minification is a process that should be done mainly for production code. It's going to be hard to work on minified files during the development process, so we need to minify our code for production code only. It is possible to enable minification in SASS or Compass compilation by adding a proper flag (`--compressed`). We will additionally use an external tool for this, to minify the code after the `uncss` process. What we need to do now is to install `gulp-clean-css`:

```
npm install --save gulp-clean-css
```

Now, minify the result of the `uncss` process. We will create a `prod` directory in which we will store our final version of the project. Now let's import `gulp-clean-css`:

```
cleanCSS = require('gulp-clean-css')
```

Let's create the sections needed in `gulpfile.js`:

```
gulp.task('clean-css-production', function () {
    return gulp.src('prod/css/main.css', {read: false})
        .pipe(rimraf({force: true}));
});

gulp.task('sass-production',['clean-css-production'], function () {
    return gulp.src('src/sass/main.sass')
        .pipe(sass().on('error', sass.logError))
        .pipe(uncss({
            html: ['prod/**/*.html']
        }))
        .pipe(cleanCSS())
        .pipe(gulp.dest('prod/css/'));
});

gulp.task('jade-production', function() {
    return gulp.src('src/jade/templates/*.jade')
        .pipe(jade())
        .pipe(gulp.dest('prod/'));
});

gulp.task('production',['jade-production', 'sass-production']);
```

Final automatizer

Now we have to gather all our previously created tasks into one file. The core of the `gulp` project is two files: `package.json`, which gathers all project dependencies, and `gulpfile`, in which you can store all tasks. Here are the tasks:

File name is: `package.json`

```
{
  "name": "automatizer",
  "version": "1.0.0",
  "description": "CSS automatizer",
  "main": "gulpfile.js",
  "author": "Piotr Sikora",
  "license": "ISC",
  "dependencies": {
    "gulp": "latest",
    "gulp-clean-css": "latest",
    "gulp-jade": "latest",
```

```
    "gulp-rimraf": "latest",
    "gulp-sass": "latest",
    "gulp-uncss": "latest",
    "gulp-util": "latest",
    "rimraf": "latest"
  }
}
```

File name is: `gulpfile.json`

```
var gulp = require('gulp'),
    sass = require('gulp-sass'),
    jade = require('gulp-jade'),
    gutil = require('gulp-util'),
    uncss = require('gulp-uncss'),
    rimraf = require('gulp-rimraf'),
    cleanCSS = require('gulp-clean-css');

gulp.task('clean-css-dist', function () {
    return gulp.src('dist/css/main.css', {read: false})
        .pipe(rimraf({force: true}));
});

gulp.task('clean-css-test', function () {
    return gulp.src('test/css/main.css', {read: false})
        .pipe(rimraf({force: true}));
});

gulp.task('sass',['clean-css-dist'], function () {
    return gulp.src('src/sass/main.sass')
        .pipe(sass().on('error', sass.logError))
        .pipe(gulp.dest('dist/css/'));
});

gulp.task('jade', function() {
    return gulp.src('src/jade/templates/*.jade')
        .pipe(jade())
        .pipe(gulp.dest('dist/'));
});

gulp.task('jade-test', function() {
    return gulp.src('src/jade/templates/*.jade')
        .pipe(jade())
        .on('error', gutil.log)
        .pipe(gulp.dest('test/'));
```

```
});

gulp.task('sass-test',['clean-css-test'], function () {
    return gulp.src('src/sass/main.sass')
        .pipe(sass().on('error', sass.logError))
        .pipe(gulp.dest('test/css/'));
});

gulp.task('uncss',['jade-test', 'sass-test'], function () {
    return gulp.src('test/css/main.css')
        .pipe(uncss({
            html: ['test/**/*.html']
        }))
        .pipe(gulp.dest('test/uncss'));
});

gulp.task('clean-css-production', function () {
    return gulp.src('prod/css/main.css', {read: false})
        .pipe(rimraf({force: true}));
});

gulp.task('sass-production',['clean-css-production'], function () {
    return gulp.src('src/sass/main.sass')
        .pipe(sass().on('error', sass.logError))
        .pipe(uncss({
            html: ['prod/**/*.html']
        }))
        .pipe(cleanCSS())
        .pipe(gulp.dest('prod/css/'));
});

gulp.task('jade-production', function() {
    return gulp.src('src/jade/templates/*.jade')
        .pipe(jade())
        .pipe(gulp.dest('prod/'));
});

gulp.task('production',['jade-production', 'sass-production']);

gulp.task('default', function () {
    gulp.watch('src/sass/*.sass', ['sass']);
    gulp.watch('src/jade/*.jade', ['jade']);
});
```

Summary

In this chapter, we discussed the basics of the Jade templating system. We saw how to append it to the frontend developer's workflow. Based on the templating system, you can now include UnCSS to your process and remove unnecessary code from the CSS file. Then we minified the final result and created a production code.

You can treat this automatizer as a starter for your projects and you can adjust it for your projects. You can also add new features and work on its evolution.

Index

www.ingramcontent.com/pod-product-compliance
Lightning Source LLC
Chambersburg PA
CBHW062052050326
40690CB00016B/3070